S0-AEV-535

The Raft of Mohammed

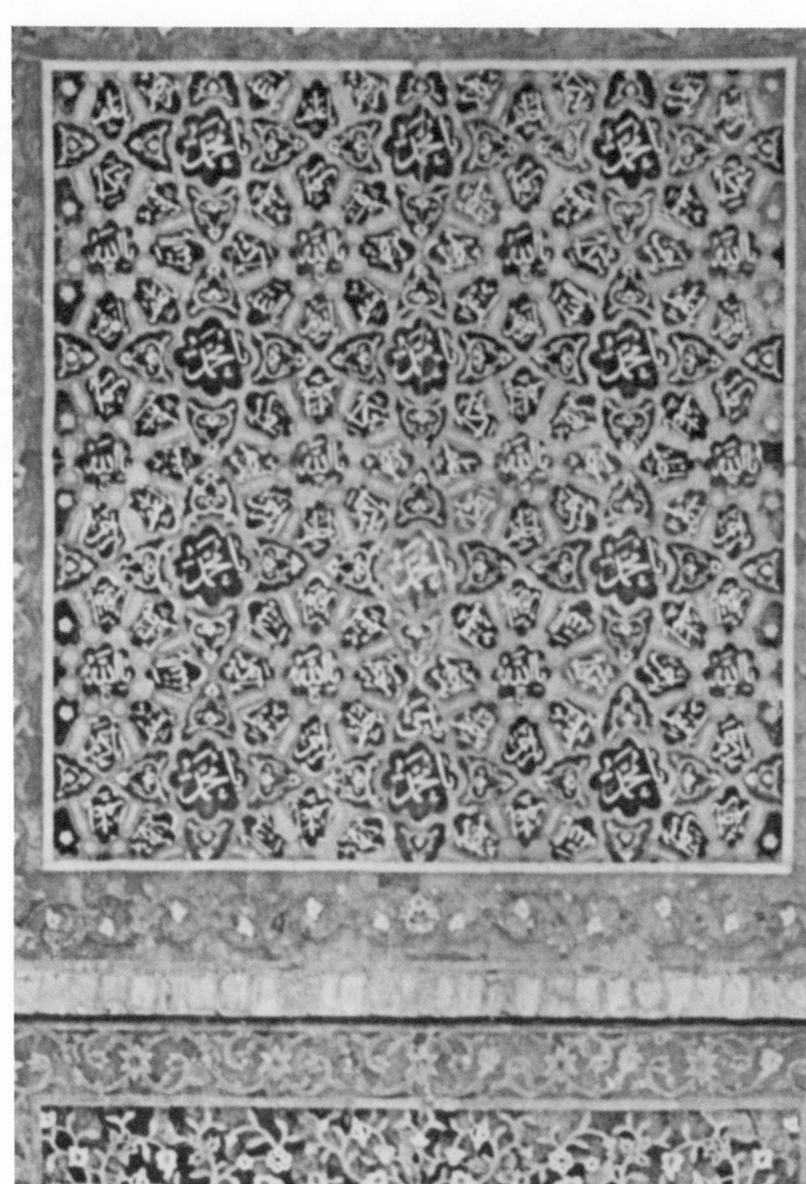

The Raft of Mohammed

Social and Human Consequences of the Return to Traditional Religion in the Arab World

Jean-Pierre Péroncel-Hugoz

Translated by George Holoch
With an Introduction by Caroline Williams

PARAGON HOUSE PUBLISHERS
New York

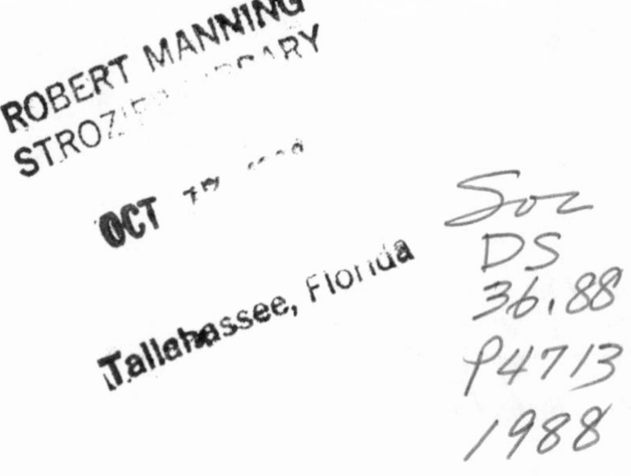

First English translation published by

Paragon House Publishers
90 Fifth Avenue
New York, New York 10011

First published in the French language
under the title *Le radeau de Mahomet*

Library of Congress Cataloging-in-Publication Data

Péroncel-Hugoz, Jean-Pierre, 1940–
The raft of Mohammed.

Translation of: Le radeau de Mahomet.
Bibliography: p.
Includes index.
1. Civilization, Arab—20th century.
2. Islam—20th century. I. Title.
DS36.88.P4713 1987 909′.04927′082 86–30306
ISBN 0–913729–31–0

To Mrs. Jihan Sadat, widow of Anwar Sadat and H. H. Shenuda III, pope of the Egyptian Coptic Orthodox Church

Table of Contents

Preface

The rise of Muslim fundamentalism in the contemporary Arab-Islamic world, in general, and its attitudes toward minorities, in particular are the subject of this book. Jean Pierre Péroncel-Hugoz, a journalist for *Le Monde* of Paris, has been studying this phenomenon since his assignment to Egypt from 1973 to 1981. In addition, the author has been awarded diplomas from institutes of higher studies in Paris, Algeria and Geneva for his work in political science, Islamic history and International Studies. Thus, he is qualified, both in theoretical background and in practical experience, to deal with this complicated subject, with its many troubling questions.

Péroncel-Hugoz discusses Islamic fundamentalism in terms of its main aspects: the religious and the political. In its religious sense, Islamic fundamentalism is described as 1) a literal return to the *shari'a,* or Islamic Law based on the Qur'an, the Book of God as revealed to His messenger Mohammed, last of the Prophets in the Abrahamic line, during 610–632 A.D.; and 2) to the *Sunna,* the practise of the Prophet, and the early (and for some, also the later) generations of Muslims, as interpreted by scholars. Politically, the author is most concerned with the Islamic fundamentalism of recent examples: the Muslim Brotherhood, founded in Egypt in 1928 by Hasan al-Banna (one of whose spiritual descendants assassinated Anwar al-Sadat in 1981), and the 1978 revolution in Iran, led by Ayatollah Khomeini. The touchstone against which Péroncel-Hugoz defines, measures and exposes Islamic fundamentalism, both as a political and a spiritual phenomenon, is the U.N. Declaration of Universal Human Rights of 1948. It is to this that he compares fundamentalist Muslim viewpoints of women —their social, political and sexual condition; of non-Muslims —mainly Jews and Christians, especially the Copts of Egypt; and of slavery. The author sees fundamentalism as a pervasive force in the Muslim world, one likely to win the day. In a final invitation, he summons all—especially foreign scholars and professionals in this field of study—to join in a stand, an outcry against Islamic fundamentalism. To this end, he provides arguments from his personal experiences and observations.

It was in Egypt, in 1975, that Péroncel-Hugoz first became aware of fundamentalism; consequently, Egyptian Muslim society receives the most criticism. He displays a warm sympathy for the Coptic Christians. The Copts, whose name derives from Qibt, the Arabic rendering of the Greek word *Aigyptos,* are descended from the native Egyptian inhabitants of the country. By the time of the Muslim conquest in 641 A.D. they had all converted to Christianity, although the native Church was at odds with the orthodox Church of Constantinople and Rome. Faced with theological nonconformity, the Byzantine Empire resorted to punitive measures and harsher taxation against its Egyptian subjects. Hence the Copts welcomed the Arab Muslim armies, in some ways they facilitated the conquest, and after it, they collaborated with the conquerors. No overt pressure was placed on them to convert to Islam. They were "people of the book" and part of the Abrahamic prophetic tradition. As long as they paid their taxes, they were well treated and they even flourished. In the early dynasties (641–1171), the Copts, clerks and functionaries of great skill became a necessary part of the bureaucracy, and as individuals they often rose to positions of great distinction.

Islam has not treated its subject peoples any more harshly or cruelly than have other dominant religions treated their minorities. Many authorities, e.g. the Copt historian S. A. Atiya, argue that it has been better. Still, their position was officially inferior to that of the Muslims, and there have been times of great difficulty for the Copts. This was so during the reign of the Shi'i Fatimid Caliph al-Hakim bi-'Amr Allah (386–411A.H./ 996–1021 A.D.), who has been acknowledged by historians as having been psychotic. In fits and rages he persecuted many of his subjects, Jews, Christians, women, even Muslims, in arbitrary ways. It was so during the Crusades, when the Muslims were battling to remove Christian invaders from their soil; and during the later Middle Ages under the Mamluks (1260–1517), whose aristocracy was a dynasty of imported slave origin, of varied ethnic and religious origins, who had nothing in common with the Egyptian citizenry except the sometimes tenuous bond of Islam, and the need to extract as much money from them as possible. Times were hard for all then.

Today, the Copts number about ten percent of all Egyptians; a skillful, energetic, and relatively well-educated minority. Their position seems to rise and fall with every change in Egyptian politics. Since they have no admixture of Arab blood and see their identity as bound up with that of Egypt, they flourished under the pro–Egyptian Wafd party, were on the outside in Abd al-Nasser's policy of pan-Arabism, and welcomed the return of Egyptian nationalism under Anwar al-Sadat. Because they were a solid constituency for this policy, Sadat treated them with none of the coldness and suspicion that Abd al-Nasser had shown them, and even appeared in public with the Copt patriarch, who bears the title Pope of Alexandria. The new Patriarch, Shenuda, was an eloquent preacher with an enthusiastic following, especially among the younger monks, and he rewarded his keenest monastic adherents by making them bishops, (who then outvoted the seasoned senior bishops of the synod in support of his policies). Observers agree that Shenuda was the most political pope that the Church of Alexandria had seen in centuries. He seemed to want an international role, and being well aware of how powerful an ally the Church of Rome could be, he suggested that the 1,400-year-old schism with Rome was on the verge of being healed and that the churches would be reunited. (Later he revoked this to the point of ordering that Catholics who married Copts would have to be rebaptised in order for a wedding to take place.)

By example and preaching, Shenuda urged the Copts to stand up for their rights and resist discrimination. Here, however, he ran against the growing Muslim movement, which feared that Sadat's policy was secularist and that the separate peace with Israel, though popular, would isolate Egypt from the Muslim world. The Copts were an accessible target. What then happened was tragic: Shenuda urged his minority to fight force with force. It was not the counsel of the Gospels and it certainly was not prudent. In the end, Sadat, after consulting Copt leaders, decided not to depose Shenuda, but to banish him to the desert monastery where he began religious life. It is this situation that Péroncel-Hugoz explores and he is clearly sympathetic with Shenuda.

Official Egypt is very resistant to any attempt to internationalize the situation of the Copts; they are seen as a peculiar problem in the Egyptian soul and body politic. Those who seek to do research among them are likely to be asked to leave the country, as Péroncel-Hugoz eventually was.

The author is both attracted and repelled by the strength and "density" of Islamic faith, and he is acutely aware that the Islamic World no longer will be subordinated to the colonial domination which began with Napoleon's invasion of Egypt in 1798 and ended with the Arab oil embargo that took place in the Egyptian–Israeli war of 1973. Since that time, the entire equation of Islamic-Western relations has dramatically changed. Rulers who failed to understand it have been overthrown, and Muslims have sought *en masse* to invoke the profound powers of religion to gain control first of their own souls, and then of their societies and their inheritance. This is the truth that Péroncel-Hugoz has seen. But is is also a truth subject to multiple interpretations.

It is important to stress and to understand that the view he expresses is only one—an immediate, pessimistic one—of what is shaking the Arab-Islamic world today. Péroncel-Hugoz argues that Arab-Islamic civilization, moribund since the 16th century, is today only a "beautiful corpse." He sees in the revival of Islam only death. Others, however, see life in this revival. They liken it to a sleeping princess, who is just now awakening from the curse laid on her by the wicked witch of the West. In this optimistic, long-range perspective, Islamic fundamentalism is viewed as a groping return to the basics, the essentials, the authenticities of Islam, and a turning away from the alien, imposed, domination of a West which is itself reproached by many of its own best minds for being spiritually bankrupt and morally irresponsible. This irreversible revolution can also be seen as a historical watershed every bit as significant as the French Revolution. We shall never again see 1948, the year in which the U.N. Declaration on Human Rights was promulgated. New "certainties" replace old. Leaders like President Reagan may damn, for example, the neo-Islamic government of Iran, but like him, they will be forced into the embarrassment of dealing with it openly or covertly.

We would do well to arm ourselves with knowledge about the interesting times in which we live. Péroncel-Hugoz provides one version, grounded in a traditional French interpretation of Islam; the bibliographic sources he cites and includes are all French. For readers who are provoked or stimulated to read more about the currents in this area, extensive literature is available in English on the modern Islamic World. For example, the prophetic *Islam in Modern History,* by Wilfred Cantwell Smith; the books of John Esposito, which make available in translation the *Voices of Resurgent Islam* or *Islam in Transition;* Hamed Enayat's *Modern Islamic Political Thought;* or Yvonne Haddad's *Contemporary Islam and the Challenge of History,* to name a few. Intercultural perceptions and ecumenical dialogue are difficult and perilous, even when interchange and friendship are their goal. If this book excites inquiry, then an important end will be achieved.

Caroline Williams
University of Texas, Austin

CHAPTER ONE

The Professional Turks

In the early nineteenth century, the Marseille traders living precariously in the Regency of Algiers gave the name of "professional Turks" to those Europeans who, to protect themselves from the outbreaks of hostility of which the *giaurs* were from time to time the targets, converted to Islam.

Today, in the West, one could give the name "professional Muslims" to the daily increasing cohort of Orientalists, genuine or specious—professors, politicians, priests, journalists, diplomats—who take advantage of the propaganda budgets of most Arab states to enjoy receptions, scholarships, conferences, junkets, symposia, and seminars. They are far from unanimous in having felt obliged to pronounce the *shahada* before a shaykh—"There is no god but Allah and Mohammed is the messenger of Allah"—a simple declaration of faith that makes you a Muslim in less time than it takes to say the words. Nor are they all by any means scribblers or impostors.

Most of them, however, have felt obliged, in writing or speaking about Islam, the Muslim world, or the Arabs, to adopt an attitude in which an excess of reverence, deliberate omissions, or worse, distortion or servility, have damaged truth, scholarship, and most seriously mutual understanding between Muslims and non–Muslims. With the exception of men like Qadhafi, contemporary Muslim political leaders never require or even suggest that European or American scholars of Islam adopt the religion of Mohammed or present a version of it in the West for the use of unbelievers. Muslims like Islamic civilization as it is. What they expect from their Western "friends," scholars, clergymen, those in favor of dialogue, is that they accept and have the unbelievers of Europe and America accept that they have to accommodate themselves to Islam, including those aspects of it that are contrary to our ideals. As for the existence of fundamentalism, theoretically it should be no more troubling for someone presenting Islamic civilization than the *gulag* is for someone wishing to inform others about Russia and the Russians without confusing them with the aberrations of the Soviet system. In fact, the situation is a little more delicate, because Communism does not have the direct and, as it were, consubstantial connection with the Russian nation that the Arabs and most other Islamic peoples have with the religion of Mohammed. It is often difficult to draw a sharp distinction between the fundamentalism embodied by the Muslim brotherhood and other extremists on the one hand, and the simple traditionalism of the Muslim in the street or the *ulama* of al-Azhar University on the other. Islamic militants naturally take full advantage of the complex interconnections between mere conservatism and fundamentalism properly speaking.

There are, however, permanent and specific Muslim virtues—faith and confidence in God, an absence of guilt about sensuality, a gift and a taste for poetry, stoicism in the face of adversity and death—that should allow for a presentation of Islamic civilization in a light that is as favorable as it is true, while not concealing its recurrent tendency toward fundamentalism.

Wouldn't the best means of respecting the "dignity" (a constantly recurring word) of the Muslims be to try to present them as they are and not as they ought to be according to our own criteria? The fact remains that, with a few notable exceptions—among the French, we would particularly mention Maxime Rodinson who, without being disingenuous, has managed to deny neither his atheism, his Marxism, nor his Jewish heritage, while simultaneously presenting a powerful and truthful vision of Islam, full of warmth and understanding—modern Orientalists often confuse sympathy or indulgence with servility. It is the worst sin an intellectual can commit, because it implies falsification.

Jacques Berque is one of the major Orientalists of the century, now seen primarily as a specialist of the Arab world. In his *Egypt: Imperialism and Revolution*,[1] nearly 300 pages are devoted to the period 1925–1950 during which the Islamic "Holy Brotherhood" was already shaking the columns of the temple. Berque, who is nevertheless very attentive to all the other underground Egyptian currents, is content with a dozen passing mentions of the Muslim brotherhood. This lacuna can in fact be explained by an error of understanding on the part of the scholar who, writing after Nasser's terrible anti–Islamic repression, no doubt believed that the Muslim brotherhood would disappear from the Arab-Islamic future.

But there were no excuses, and in any event not those of ignorance or defective judgment, when no fewer than fourteen French researchers published a *summa* on *Syria Today*,[2] the fruit of several years of fieldwork during the 1970s, in which the Muslim brotherhood, growing strongly from Aleppo to Damascus after having been banned by the Syrian government in 1963, was briefly mentioned seven times in passing in more than 450 pages. This is comparable to a study of present–day Spain that would neglect the subject, an equally thorny one to be sure, of Opus Dei.

While pursuing a contrary aim to that of some of their predecessors of the colonial period who sought to blacken Islam, contemporary writers have attained the identical result: the presentation of a deformed and sometimes even caricatural image of the religion and its believers. This Islam seen through rose colored glasses can finally be more pernicious, the source of even more misunderstandings than the slanderous procedure of a certain earlier Orientalism that was primarily concerned with justifying colonization.

When one learns that Louis-Antoine Pavy, Bishop of Algiers under Napoleon III, thundered from his pulpit: "The Koran is an absurdity!"; when one glances through *The Anti-Koran or Mohammedanism Condemned by Itself*[3] by Jean-Marie Aarfi, a "converted Turk," it suffices to open Islam's holy book to be convinced that the text and the religion that grew from it are great, even if we are far from accepting all the postulates of the one and all the practices of the other.

On the other hand, when I hear that "the dynamism of Islam lies above all in the permanent Islamization which consists of respecting the spirit, not the letter;" that "the spirit of Islam is fundamentally democratic;" that "Arab women are as free as we are;" that "Koranic law is in many respects less restrictive than we think;" that "Islam properly understood does not oppress women, but is rather a means of advancement;" that Islam "has never been imposed by force anywhere;" finally that Islam is "progressive," that it is, par excellence, the religion of a "personal effort of reflection," of "humanism," "tolerance," "equality," "change," "socialism," in short the champion of all our Westerners' fantasies; when I see a major program on French television on the Black slave trade with not a word about the Arab-Muslim role in what Senghor has called "the greatest genocide in history;" when I hear repeated endlessly the fable, perhaps to charm our last surviving anticlericals, that "Islam is a religion without priests;" when I bear all that in mind and then discover in the field, sharing the daily life of Muslims, that their doctors of the faith and their politicians, sometimes to a tragic extent, give primacy to the letter over the spirit of the Koran; that the permanently wretched of the Arab East are indeed women, peasants, and religious or ethnic minorities; that the shaykhs, muftis, and *ulama* of Sunnism and the mullahs, *hojatolislams,* and *ayatollahs* of Shi'ism are indeed the equivalents of our priests, bishops and theologians, while Muslim theology represents acres of exegesis; that most "progressive" Islamic regimes are without any possible doubt what Jacques Berque calls "a socialist form of misery," then I begin to rebel, to have the impression that I have been duped.

It has often been observed among young French volunteer workers who came to serve in the Maghrib or the Mashrig, full of good will for the peoples of the regions and carrying no intellectual baggage on the subject but a few little books and articles that painted an idyllic picture, that within a few months, after the discovery of a different reality, they experienced a strong feeling of disappointment, even of hostility, toward the Muslims, as though they had been deceived by them. In fact they were deceived by those who, a few thousand miles away, in the comfortable unreality of their studies, draw up imaginary pictures of Islam in which the outline of that community is at best blurred or rearranged.

We have a whole host of voices whose single concern, when Islam is in question, is to prettify, to transform, to ameliorate, to exculpate, all at the expense of accuracy. Speaking of *The Promises of Islam*[4] by Roger Garaudy, the French-speaking Algerian scholar of Islam, Mohammed Arkoun, stigmatized this "literature which, in the guise of generosity, 'spiritual' fervor, and reaction against the injustices of the past, is in fact a continuation of colonial literature, perpetuating its intellectual failings, its contempt (no doubt unconscious here) for the real expectations of the Muslim public, and its close connection, on the other hand, with the needs of the Western public."[5] We have fallen from one excess into another, but the victims remain the same: the deceived Westerner and the caricatured Oriental.

In May 1981, when a Turkish terrorist attempted to assassinate Pope John Paul II in Rome, machinery immediately went into operation in certain publications, institutes, and associations in order that no one mention that Mehmet Ali Ağca was a Muslim, that he had in particular been active in Turkish Islamic movements, and that he had offered fundamentalist Islamic arguments to justify his crime. Radio stations and newspapers were able to announce the arrest of the perpetrator of the attempt without providing anything about his sociological background. (Others, with an opposite and equally inadmissible purpose claimed, without proof, that the assassin was a Palestinian.) There were even insinuations, expressed with many circumlocutions, that the Pope had at bottom brought about what had just happened to him by carrying out a "threatening"[6] journey to Turkey in 1979. That country, we were told, contains only a minuscule percentage of Christians, and along the way we were not reminded that Istanbul is the most prestigious seat of the Orthodox patriarchate, with which the Vatican is obliged to maintain relations if it wishes to develop the inter-Christian dialogue whose aim is not, so far as one knows, to harm Islam.

At the same time, there was no reference to the enlightening letter, so revealing about the ties of the criminal (even if he was the unwitting tool of atheist forces, that manipulation was possible only because of his religious convictions) to the Islamic fundamentalist movement, that Ali Agča, having escaped from prison where he had been confined for murdering a Turkish journalist, wrote to the Turkish daily *Milliyet* on the occasion of the papal visit to Turkey. He wanted to know what this "disguised leader of a crusade," this "spiritual leader of the West" was doing in an Islamic land. He had to be done away with if only to "make someone pay for the profanation of the mosque of Mecca organized by the United States and Israel."[7] There was a similar silence in the face of the typically fundamentalist declarations of Ali Agča after the assassination attempt: "I also wanted to kill the King of England and the President of the European Parliament, but I didn't when I learned that England had a queen and the President was a woman, because, as a Turk and a Muslim, I do not kill women."

It was not a matter, on the occasion of the Vatican assassination attempt, of putting the entire Muslim world in the dock, but simply of showing the event for what it had all the appearances of being: the first manifestation outside the Islamic world of fundamentalist violence and intolerance or, if you prefer, of the Muslim extreme right.

The most remarkable attitude of the professional Muslims is that expressed by Catholic priests and members of religious orders who attempt at any price to establish a correspondence between Islam and Christianity. To accomplish this, they are ready to do what most of their Muslim colleagues do not even wish: to remove from the religion of Christ everything excessive, everything that is thought likely to trouble their "Muslim brothers."

The Dominican father, Claude Geffré, noted for his level-headedness, in the euphoric atmosphere of the second Islamic–Christian Conference in Tunis in May 1979, went so far as to proclaim: "The revelation of which Mohammed is the messenger is a Word of God that addresses me in my faith."[8] The concession did not satisfy the Muslims, for whom Mohammed had brought "the" divine Word not "a" Word, and *stricto sensu*, it contravened Christian dogma. Two years earlier, Father Michel Lelong, then director of the Secretariat of the French Church for relations with Islam, had gone even further, decreeing: "For some it is in Jesus Christ, for others in the Koran that God has revealed Himself in His plenitude. But all (Christians and Muslims) believe—with their brothers in Judaism—that He spoke through the prophets."[9] Casually, in a great pseudo-ecumenical and openly syncretistic mishmash, this evades the divine character of Jesus, an essential article of faith for every Christian. The Son of God is reduced to the rank of a Messenger from God, which the Messiah is in fact according to Islamic doctrine. If there are Christians who really think that—and why not?—they ought to be logical with themselves and embrace Islam. It would be better for them in every respect than to become heretics without realizing it out of their urgent desire to "dialogue" with the Muslims. The fundamental difference—which no one in this world ever mentions—between the founder of Christianity and the apostles on the one hand, and the founder of Islam and his companions on the other, is that the former did not practice physical violence and did not seek temporal power, while the latter . . . .

A true Islamic–Christian dialogue will begin when each one has accepted the other as he is. From that point on, the most urgent task will be to organize and improve daily life together wherever Muslims and Christians coexist, chiefly in the Near East. This is what is important, not some hypothetical doctrinal convergence. For the moment, we are still at the level of very abstract discussions in the hothouse atmosphere of lecture rooms cut off from the rest of the world.

Father Lelong, appointed by the Vatican in 1980 to the position of "consultant" for relations with non–Christian religions, is possessed by a naiveté which approaches ferocity: "I would rather see the Christians of Lebanon dead than to know they had to kill their neighbors to survive," he said to me in early 1982. He inundates newspapers and institutions with fevered articles and petitions, never missing any of those Parisian celebrations where the "reconciliation among believers" leads to the support of any cause, provided it is "Islamic," in an atmosphere that recalls both childhood charitable festivals and the collective hallucinations of the 1950s in honor of Stalin.

But Father Lelong's case is not unique. Another Dominican, Jacques Lanfry of the diocese of Algiers, had probably never had the slightest idea of changing his religion. That did not prevent him, in a dizzying rhetorical flight, during an Islamic–Christian seminar in Tripoli, Libya in February 1976, from allowing himself publicly to ask forgiveness, "from the bottom of his heart," from the Muslims for "all the lack of respect and all the improprieties, in speech and writing, toward Mohammed, the respected prophet of Islam."

After all, why not? Why not recognize what exists? Mohammed has often been caricatured in the West; emphasis has been placed on his Napoleonic side—the love of women, war, and power—at the expense of his spiritual dimension. In the middle of a century that was deferential toward Islam, Voltaire produced *Fanatacism, or Mohammed the Prophet,* a tragedy in five acts, containing the lines: "Impostor in Mecca and prophet in Medina, he has persuaded thirty nations to adore the very infamies that we detest."

Father Lanfry's repentance was unfortunately unilateral. It was naturally greeted with enthusiasm in an atmosphere that was heavily influenced by Colonel Qadhafi's presence at the conference. Spread by radios and newspapers throughout the Islamic world, it appeared to the more moderate Muslims both as a recognition of Christian wrongs against the Prophet and as proof that the Muslim world has nothing to reproach itself with as far as Christendom is concerned, since there had been nothing demanded in exchange for such an unprecedented declaration. The unfortunate ecclesiastic was very badly rewarded for his efforts, since the Algerian authorities later expelled him from his beloved Kabylia, suspecting that he might provide cultural support to the Berbers who were struggling against Arabization.

But what an idea to hold a meeting under the aegis of Colonel Qadhafi, the militant supporter of holy war. Anticipating the trap, the World Council of Churches of Geneva, several Orthodox Churches, including that of Egypt, and even the very traditional Islamic University of Cairo, al-Azhar, sent no representatives. Of the fourteen members of the official Catholic delegation, only two were Arabs, one of whom, Father Georges Anawati, an old Egyptian Dominican scholar, was the only one experienced in dialogues with Muslims. On the Islamic side, apart from the Sunni shaykh Subhi Salih, vice–mufti of Lebanon, known for his knowledge of Arabic and French culture and his relative freedom of mind, there were aligned bureaucrats loyal to Qadhafi or folkloric figures: the Afghan imam of the mosque of Copenhagen, the president of a Muslim association of Nairobi, and the like.

The Christians were properly thanked for their conciliatory tendencies. The Colonel-President came in person to suggest that the participants "recommend the recognition of Mohammed as Prophet." "This request is absurd and anachronistic," in the judgment of the modernist Muslim scholar Mohamed Arkoun.[10] It is above all unacceptable because it would be equivalent to a suicide by the Church. Qadhafi and other Islamic activists who complain about the Christians in these terms: "We recognize the Messiah while they stubbornly refuse to recognize the Prophet," know perfectly well that their argument is specious. The Koran presents Jesus as a "messenger of God," like Moses or Mohammed, and to profess that is not, for a Muslim, to abjure his faith, quite the contrary. But if a Christian agrees that Mohammed is a prophet, the last of a series that includes Jesus, who is therefore not the Son of God, there is no longer any reason for him not to convert to Islam.

As a crowning touch, the delegates of the Holy See, who must have been unaware of an article published in the Bulletin of the Tripoli Seminar that asserted: "The defeat of the Vatican is certain; through this dialogue, it is seeking a way of preserving the Catholic believers that it still has," allowed themselves, in the fatigue of the conclusion of the discussions, to swallow extremist propositions of Qadhafi concerning the resolution of the Israeli–Palestinian question.

Pope Paul VI had to disavow his representatives. A single small satisfaction for the Christians was the adoption of a recommendation, which disturbed the supporters of holy war in the Near East, on "the necessity of declaring and defending religious freedom." The real lesson they ought to have derived from this congress of fools, aside from the fact that, when there are wrongs on both sides, it serves no purpose to be the only one who says *mea culpa, mea maxima culpa,* is that the problem of the Muslim world confronted with a dialogue with Christendom is the absence among the Muslim intelligentsia, religious or secular, of systematic study of Christianity, the lack of an "Occidentalism."

Almost all contemporary Muslim thinkers have the knowledge of and prejudices about Christianity and the Christians that a nineteenth century French clergyman must have had about the Muslim world. There are naturally some shining exceptions, but the influence of their thought is all the more minimal in the Muslim world because many of them, censored or misunderstood at home, are forced to publish abroad (often in French), or even to go into exile.

Marcel Boisard, the Swiss secretary general of the International Association Islam et Occident, discovered in 1981 that, "in a European country" that he did not identify "ways of talking about Islam and the Muslims have changed neither in substance nor in form since 1945." This former representative of the Red Cross in Egypt could have simultaneously recalled that the clichés about Christians have hardly varied in the Near east since the year 1000. The encouragement by every means of the development of an "Occidentalism" in the Muslim world should be the primary duty of every Christian in contact with that world, Edward Said to the contrary notwithstanding.[11]

The tactic of the professionals of dialogue, then, consists of "making Islam feel confident," and every time the opportunity arises, stuffing the two religions into the same bag. Thus, for instance, Father Lelong informs us, that "although it is true that Christianity and Islam have too often been used to crush women, we must recognize that they have also helped to improve their condition," and so on. The trick is played. Whoever is unaware that even in the worst of Christian societies the situation of women has been no doubt less harsh than in the best of Islamic societies, will search his soul and no longer dare to cast a reproving eye on those who deprive Muslim women of their freedom.[12]

Other Christians think they can charm the Muslims by expressing indignation whenever the subject of the Crusades arises. To be sure, they were not holy, but each of them over the course of 350 years had participants who were moved more by faith than by the lust for money or power. The Muslims themselves have at their disposal this declaration by Mohammed which would, at the least, allow for the absolution of the Franks: "A single just man in a pilgrimage redeems the rest of the pilgrims."

Our Crusades have been considered, from beginning to end, abominable and unjustifiable, while the same accusers find it thoroughly normal that the Muslims are ready to destroy Israel in order to recapture Jerusalem, which is merely their third holy city after Mecca and Medina, or that they are ready to carry on a holy war if those two cities are occupied or simply threatened. Former Algerian president Ben Bella presents his "considered judgment": "If there is no other solution, then let nuclear war come, and let us have done once and for all [with Israel]"[13]

How many times since the memorable Tripoli conference of 1976 have Catholics in the Near East heard Muslims say to them in complete good faith: "Your Pope has recognized that you have wronged us." It is impossible to explain that the initiative and zeal of a simple priest, caught up in the vertigo of dialogue at any price, were purely individual. Father Lanfry made the single error of not proposing that his apology be balanced by a corresponding gesture on the Muslim side for the lies and mockery spread among the Arabs on the subject of Christianity and the Christians.

Let us leave aside the accusations of several *suras* of the Koran which no one in the Muslim world can ever openly put in question, one of the harshest being that the people of the Book—Jews and Christians—"knowingly altered" the Scriptures in order to prevent anyone from reading the announcement of the coming of Mohammed, the seal of the prophets. Let us just glance rapidly at what is published and said today in Muslim countries about Christians and even about Christ. "Faith in God is shared by you Christians and the idolators, while the Muslim faith does not resemble the Christian faith" (official journal of al-Azhar University, 1979); "The Crusades, which began eight hundred years ago, are continuing . . . the Church will never authorize Christians to rent an apartment or a shop to a Muslim, and those who do so will be excommunicated" (*What Every Muslim Should Know About Christianity and Religious Missions,* by Ibrahim Ghabhan (Riyadh, 1977), also distributed in Egypt and Sudan); "the Nazarenes (believers in Jesus of Nazareth) are cannibals; they eat the body of God and adore a lamb" (typical sermon recorded in different mosques in Egypt from 1979 to 1981).

The Christians of the Near East pretend not to hear, even when a loudspeaker carries the insults into their own houses. A recent case nevertheless provoked a reaction. Shaykh Mitwalli Sha'rawi is a popular preacher much appreciated in Egypt. A former minister of religious affairs, he is nonetheless not a tool of the authorities, even having had the nerve to refuse the honor of being a senator that Sadat had conferred on him. Early in 1981, in one of his television talks, he approached the subject of Christ. Recognized as a prophet by Mohammed, the Messiah, in principle, has nothing to fear from a Muslim. Indeed, Ahmad Shawqi (1868–1932), the most widely read Arabic poet of this century, did not hesitate to write: "With the birth of Jesus, birth of Gentleness, noble human Virtues, light of hearts, Modesty. . . . Neither threats, nor violence in words, nor vengeance, nor sword, nor conquest, nor spilling of blood."

But there is a point in the life of Christ that has never failed to disturb Muslims, in whose eyes "marriage is half of religion." At thirty-three, the Savior was still unmarried. As a general rule, their theologians deal with the question by recalling that this serious defect will be repaired by the marriage of Jesus to a fertile Muslim woman on his return to earth on the eve of the end of the world. The problem has also troubled Eastern Christians, notably the Copts, who are very insistent on the necessity of marriage. This no doubt explains their rather distorted interpretation of the relations between Christ and a certain Salome recounted in apocryphal texts like the Gospel of Saint Thomas discovered at Nag–Hammadi in the middle of this century.

"Well, my dear brothers, Christ did not marry because he was impotent," Shaykh Sha'rawi suddenly asserted in front of millions of television viewers. Whether the explanation satisfied Muslims or left them unconvinced, among Christians it took on the character of a final humiliation. The macho instincts of the Copts were frustrated by the legal impossibility of their replying by formulating the slightest reservation on the personality of Mohammed, even in a humorous vein. The pressure of Christian opinion finally was so great that the Church hierarchies asked the Minister of Information to assure that Sha'rawi "no longer dealt on television with a religion that was not his own." The excessively imaginative preacher was kept off the screen for a while, but Father Bulus Bassili, a Coptic priest who was for long a pro–government representative from a large, mostly Christian, poor neighborhood of Cairo, was thrown in prison on Sadat's orders, simultaneously with members of the political opposition of all varieties, in September 1981, for having tape-recorded a speech refuting Sha'rawi's arguments. The recording that circulated among the Copts had had a calming effect, but while any shaykh could use television to attack what Christians hold most dear, a priest had no right to comfort his flock, even in private.

More often than not, Muslim misstatements about Christianity derive much more from ignorance than from malice. The problem is that when one suggests to Muslims that they should learn about Christian doctrine or read the Bible, in general they refuse categorically, "since everything is in the Koran." The Pope of Alexandria, patriarchs of Antioch or Babylon, Melkite or Roman priests, Coptic monks of the Egyptian desert, and the Maronite monks of Kaslik all know the Koran, sometimes better than many shaykhs. But in the eyes of the latter, to open the Gospels would be a loss of dignity. As a result, despite the incompleteness of the knowledge Near Eastern Christians have about Islam, they know much more about it than Muslims know about Christianity. The papal university of Lebanon is open to Muslims; al-Azhar in Cairo is closed to Egyptian Christians, even for the study of secular disciplines.

The determination of certain Westerners to serve Islam by any means sometimes produces absurd situations. Eva de Vitray–Meyerovitch is a woman who became a Muslim and went to Mecca. She had every right to do so, and it is a matter of little import. One might be a bit surprised—since religion is a private matter in France—that she allows her new status to be used as a banner: "Eva de Vitray–Meyerovitch, a Frenchwoman converted to Islam, is going to speak to you." She is known among students of Islam in France for having edited an anthology of Muslim mystical writings.

In February and October 1980, she published two articles in *Le Monde,* in which, to sum them up, she declared, with the support of quotations from the Koran, on the one hand that the principle of holy war is above all psychological, and on the other that "the severity of corporal punishment in Muslim law has a purely deterrent character: it is a sword of Damocles that it is almost impossible to use." This second point collapsed of its own weight, coinciding as it did with yet another public stoning to death, in Iran, of four people accused respectively of prostitution, adultery, homosexuality, and pandering.

As for the first point, it would have been enough to have glanced at any of a number of Islamic magazines, fundamentalist or simply traditionalist, published in Egypt or the Arabian peninsula, or to have listened to sermons in Near Eastern mosques since 1975, to see that the *jihad* is defined as above all "physical." "Pagan" Black Africa, a reputedly easy prey, and in general whatever is not the *dar al-Islam*—literally the "house of Islam"—that is, the *dar al-harb* (the "territory of war"), also known as *dar al-kufr* ("territory of unbelief"), or *dar al-jahiliya* ("territory of ignorance") is doomed sooner or later to be the target of the holy war. Even a moderate Muslim like Nasser was no doubt thinking along these lines when he wrote in *Philosophy of the Revolution:* "It is impossible for us to evade the task of expanding our civilization, even to the center of the [African] virgin forest." With his money, plots, and Islamic Legion, this is what Colonel Qadhafi is attempting to bring about, in his own way, from Chad to the Central African Republic and Senegal.

The "epistle" of the Andalusian jurist Ibn Abi Zayd El-Qayrawani (922-996) devoted to the "elements of the dogma and the law of Islam according to the Malikite rite,"[14] published in Arabic and French in Algiers in 1975, and since then distributed widely among the Muslims of France, envisages only one *jihad,* accompanied by "hostilities," although it recommends that they not be begun "before having called on the enemy to embrace the religion of Allah." The Syrian theoretician Ahmad Ibn Taymiyya (1263–1328), author of a *Treatise of Public Law,* is if not the father of all Muslim fundamentalism, at least the supreme reference of modern Islamic fundamentalists from Pakistan to Morocco. He defined the *jihad* as "the best form of voluntary service that man offers to God." The fundamentalist group that spawned Khalid Istambuli, the twenty–four year old lieutenant who led the assassins of Sadat on October 6, 1981, had chosen the name al–Jihad.

Its "thinker," the electronic engineer Abd al-Salam Faraj, had his head filled by Ibn Taymiyya and his distant Pakistani disciple Abu'l-Ala Mawdudi (1903–1979), promoter of the ideology of the noose and the whip dear to the officers of Islamabad. In his pamphlet *The Missing Obligation,*[15] Faraj added to the five classic pillars of Islam (the declaration of faith, prayer five times a day, daytime fasting and chasity during the month of Ramadan, ritual charity and, if possible, pilgrimage to Mecca) a sixth imperative, holy war, going so far as to assert: "It is a bad reason to delay the *jihad* on the pretext of increasing one's learning." Shaykh Umar Abd al-Rahman, a professor at al–Azhar, chosen in spring 1981 as "amir, mufti, and *ulama*" by the members of al–Jihad, provided them with a *fatwa* (religious decision in conformity with Islamic law) asserting that "it is appropriate to despoil the impious in order to finance the holy war." Thus, a few weeks before Sadat's assassination, six Coptic artisan–jewellers of the little town of Nag–Hammadi were robbed and murdered.

To be sure, the whole Muslim world does not approve these incitements to crime and rapine. To be sure, if one looks carefully, one can find Muslim texts or theologians that describe a psychological *jihad.* But it is false and dangerous to assert that this is now the dominant tendency; it has, moreover always been a minority tendency in Islamic lands, outside a few philosophical circles. The image of the *jihad* that is now dominant among the young in the Arab–Muslim world, even among those who are not involved in extremism and who hardly seem inclined to engage in warfare to expand the *dar al–Islam,* is that of armed confrontation.

In the footnotes of her first article, Mme de Vitray-Meyerovitch referred to herself as a "member of C.N.R.S. in Paris" and "former professor at the University of al-Azhar." I admit that neither I, nor anyone on my editorial staff, paid any attention to these unusual titles. But, a few weeks later, the secretary of the University of al-Azhar summoned me twice, for sessions less boring than his detractors would have led me to believe, asking for an explanation and, if possible, a correction in *Le Monde,* "no French woman nor even a European can claim to have been a professor at al-Azhar, especially in Philosophy, the department which the interested party references"! I consulted the cultural services' attaché at the French Embassy in Cairo to cross-check the criticisms of al-Azhar; they replied, "Essentially what Mme de Vitray-Meyerovitch did in Egypt in November-December 1975 was to give six lectures on the Islamic culture in French at different Egyptian universities. She has never taught there." I wrote Mme de Vitray to inform her—briefly—of our problem and to ask her, in case she should credit herself again in *Le Monde,* to please find an appropriate description of her former activities, satisfactory to herself, and in keeping with "the spirit of precision of al-Azhar and certain of our readers" and which would avoid further embarrassment for my newspaper regarding the Sorbonne of Islam. (In the meantime, we had received from various quarters other objections to this title of "former professor at al-Azhar.)

In the Spring of 1981, my office received two very dark photocopies from Mme de Vitray. One was a letter from an official of the cultural services at the French Embassy in Khartoum which said that Mme de Vitray was a "researcher at C.N.R.S." (Wouldn't it have been easier to contact the central headquarters of this organization in Paris for such proof?) The other was a certificate from the department of French at al-Azhar, indicating that Mme de Vitray had been invited there to teach, a fact no one ever contested, with the understanding that this position was temporary and did not confer upon her any title. There had also been an invitation for her to assist the Group for Research and Studies on Islamic Civilization which led her in 1981 to write on letterhead paper from the University of Paris—VII, as "co-director of G.R.E.C.I." Furthermore, in Pierre Assouline's *The New Converts,* Mme de Vitray claims another dubious title: "After the war (. . .) I was head of the department of Humanities at C.N.R.S.," etc.

In short, Eva de Vitray-Meyerovitch could never have been a professor at al-Azhar, where it is required that all the classes be taught in classic Arabic. She taught some courses, or more precisely, gave lectures, in French, to Egyptian students in Cairo, and she was at one time an employee of C.N.R.S. in Paris. This alone is impressive. But without a doubt she calculated—and she is not alone, even though her case may be a bit extreme—that by assuming a more prestigious title, which, alas! for her was undeserved, she would have a greater impact in the defense of Islam to which she so assiduously devoted herself in Paris.

Of this conniving type, our century has its Doctor Lebon, and even worse. Born in Eure-et-Loir in 1841, an amateur archeologist of Buddhist India, medical doctor in 1876, Gustave Lebon had published as early as 1868 his *Physiology of the Generation,* followed by *Practical Treatment for Genitourinary Diseases* (1869) and *Practical Hygiene for the Soldier and the Wounded,* opportunely published the year of the war of 1870. But, he has not been forgotten because of the Arabs, about whom he wrote a panegyric in 1884, re-edited many times since, at their request, and which today the princes of oil display in an expensive gold binding on the bedside tables of their distinguished French-speaking guests. However, Lebon's *Civilization of the Arabs* is not a blatant propogation of Islamic faith like most other Western works.

Another contemporary Western propagator of Islam is Dr. Maurice Bucaille, a French surgeon and author of *The Bible, the Koran, and Science,*[16] that has even been translated into Serbo–Croatian and Indonesian, though it is unknown to a broad public in Europe. The book would not call for harsh criticism were it not for the fact that it uses against Jews and Christians arguments that have been rejected by most great Muslim thinkers from Ibn Khaldun to Mohammed Abduh.

Bucaille, who discovered the Arabs and their religion only when he was around fifty, thanks to some of his Muslim patients (among whom, it seems, was King Faysal II of Saudi Arabia), asserts that he learned enough Arabic in two years to be able to read the Koran in the original. This is a miraculous achievement, and has been practically recounted as such not only in the fundamentalist Arab reviews, but also in the special information bulletins circulated in many dialects by UNESCO. This "miracle worker" is placed by the United Nations on the same level culturally as Teilhard de Chardin. But scripture experts and a variety of scholars shrugged their shoulders when reading his works, *The Bible, the Koran, and Science* and *Man: From Where Does He Originate? Answers from Science and The Holy Scriptures*. The doctor-writer declared in the *Bulletin* of UNESCO:[17] "The Koranic revelation does not contain the errors found in the Bible. . . . I have found no incorrect assertions in the Koran. . . . I have discovered that many passages of the Koran could not be the work of a man."

Benign assertions, which might only provoke surprise because they were published by a secular international organization, some of whose member states represent a billion and a half Christians, while, if I am not mistaken, none of its publications has ever expressed reservations about Islam; the slightest criticism of that religion would not have failed to provoke a typically Parisian uproar, naturally with the cooperation of our professional Muslims.

Established in Paris, directed by Francophiles since its founding in 1946, UNESCO is bound to political and religious neutrality. It is controlled by only two forces which are surprisingly not always antagonistic: American imperialism, transparently disguised in a "cultural" robe, and a more and more intransigent Islam, glorified by Western intellectuals. The strategists of the State Department have always thought that Islamism, in its extremist version, was the sure-fire antidote for communism. Zbignew Brzezinski, President Carter's National Security Advisor, had to admit outright, "Not only do we not fear the rebirth of Islam but . . . on the contrary, we welcome it." It seems that when Egypt and France got together, at the time of Valéry Giscard d'Estaing, to overthrow Qadhafi, the Libyan dictator was saved by Washington.

Until the message of enlightened Muslim theologians like the Egyptian Shaykh Amin al-Kholi[18]—who in the middle of this century disposed of any "scientific" interpretation of the Pentateuch and the Koran—has managed to be heard in the West, we will have to tolerate Dr. Bucaille and his like tracing a parallel between "the contortions, the confusion, the disorder, and the contradictions" of Jewish and Christian scriptures as opposed to the luminous explanation of all phenomena in the universe, past, present and future, contained in the Koran. We will have to listen once again to the old Islamic legend about additions, deletions and other "falsifications of the Scriptures" carried out by the Judeo–Christian world to conceal God's sending to men of the final prophet: Mohammed. The nineteenth century Egyptian religious reformer, Mohammed Abduh, while not accepting Jewish and Christian exegeses of pre–Islamic holy texts, declared that the Old and New Testaments were "authentic," considering it "impossible that Jews and Christians in all countries had all agreed to change the text."

Of Bucaille and his emulators, who are absolutely determined to make the Koran state that Mohammed, by the grace of God, announced everything in advance to humanity—electricity, bicycles, local anesthesia—there will remain, when the vogue for gimcrack exegetes has passed, at least an occasion for laughter.

NOTES

1. Paris: Gallimard, 1967.
2. Paris: Centre national de la recherche scientifique, 1980.
3. Paris: Editions Ernest Leroux, 1927.
4. Paris: Seuil, 1981.
5. *France-Pays Arabes,* no. 99, 1982.
6. Maxime Rodinson, in *Le Monde,* May 23, 1981.
7. On November 20th, 1979, a group of armed rebels, made up of four to six hundred Séoudiens and Muslims of other nationalities, including women and children, locked themselves in the Great Mosque of The Mecca—the one which contains the Kabba or Sacred Stone—and for two weeks withstood a fierce siege against the royal forces. Contrary to opinion widely held in Muslim circles, this was not the first time that the waters of Kaaba were stained with blood. In the beginning of Islamism, rebels hostile to the Omayyad dynasty of Damascus withstood a

siege within the Mosque of the mosques for eight months before surrendering. In 931, the Qarmate Shiites (names after their founder Hamdane Qarmat) seized The Mecca, removed the Black Stone (which the Muslims believed was given to Abraham by the archangel Gabriel) and kept it for several years in their capital of Mouaminieh (actually Houfouf, in eastern Arabia).

8. *Islamochristiana* (multilingual annual publication of the Pontifical Institute of Arab and Islamic Studies), Rome, 1979, vol. V.
9. *Le Monde,* April 27, 1977.
10. *Le Figaro,* February 22, 1976.
11. Edward Said, *Orientalism* (New York: Pantheon, 1978).
12. See the work by the Islamophile Egyptian woman doctor, Nawal El Saadawi, *The Hidden Face of Eve: Women in the Arab World* (Boston: Beacon Press, 1982).
13. *Politique internationale,* no. 16, Summer 1982.
14. One of the four juridical schools or rites of Sunni (or orthodox) Islam.
15. *El-Ahram,* December 14, 1981.
16. Paris: Seghers, 1976.
17. No. 45, 1982.
18. Fathers J. Jomier and R. Caspar, "L'Exégèse scientifique du Coran d'après le cheikh Amine El-Kholi," *Mélanges* de l'Institut dominicain des études orientales, vol. IV (Cairo, 1957).

CHAPTER TWO

The Holy Strike

A single proposition has always been entertained in Islamic countries, according to which, in the history of the world, there was on the one hand, the Islamic conquest, which was humane, beneficent and received with enthusiasm by the conquered peoples; on the other were invasions, colonialism, exploitation, destruction, and rivers of blood, wherever it was not Muslims who were acting and especially if the victims were Muslims. For ten years, there has not been a conference, a symposium, or a lecture dealing with Muslim history in which this myth has not been celebrated, even by Western "historians" or westernized Arab figures who have all been informed and influenced by historians of the Maghrib and the Mashriq who are above reproach, like Gaston Wiet (1887–1971), professor at the Collège de France, and Charles-André Julien (1891–), former holder of the chair of colonial history at the Sorbonne. In September 1981, on the occasion of a Western–Islamic function held in Paris, one could read: "Since the Middle Ages, the West has habitually called Islamic expansion 'conquest,' while the Arabs use '*fath*,' which means both victory and opening: the opening of the soldiers of the prophet Mohammed to the civilizations they discovered—Indian, Persian, Greek, Berber, African—opening of the peoples converted to the message of the Koran." Those who are reluctant to rely on European historians have only to open Ibn Khaldun and other good Islamic sources to see that the Arab invasions, from Egypt to Sind and Gibraltar to Palestine, were violent and destructive, like all military conquests, before bringing peace and prosperity to several countries. We will not go so far as to follow the convert to Islam, Roger Garaudy, who, in *The Promises of Islam,* lets slip this strange judgment: "The great invasions and the great dominations were always great regressions."[1] What are we to conclude about the splendid Islamic empire that extended from the Indus to Senegal?

Venerated today as a saint of Islam, Uqba, one of the Muslim conquerors of North Africa, was noted, before he was killed by Berbers, for raids against virgins, massacres of villagers, and pillage. Kusayla, prince of the Awrabas, helped by Byzantium, and Kahina, queen of the Awras, relying only on the forces of her tribe, fought with the energy of despair against the Arabs. And the North Africans converted to Islam committed apostasy "twelve times in seventy years" according to Ibn Khaldun, despite the capital punishment decreed for apostates by Koranic law, which was widely enforced in the early years of the Hegira. In India, before building Lahore, the Muslims sweeping through the land in the eleventh century established their control only through the practice of scorched earth policy.

Another excessively pious legend that deserves demolition is the one that claims that Islam had no experience of an abominable institution like the Inquisition. Not only did Muslims experience it in various forms, but this happened before the Christians, who tasted its delights beginning only in the twelfth century. In Baghdad, Caliph al-Ma'mun instituted the inquisitorial system before its codification in the *Mihna*; the jurist Ahmad Ibn Hanbal, who is still an authority twelve centuries later, was censored and put in irons. In Egypt, around the year 1000, the Fatimid dynasty pursued, with sword and whip, all Sunnis who were opposed to state–sponsored Shi'ism.[2] In a general way, the Shi'ite–Sunni conflicts resemble in many details our wars of religion. The Almohads (1130–1269), in the Maghrib and Andalusia, were particularly intransigent on inter–Muslim doctrinal points; the celebrated philosopher Averroes was shabbily exiled for "heresy," and his treatises were publicly destroyed in Cordoba.

After the works of Louis Massignon, one can no longer ignore the torture of the mystic al–Hallaj who, under the Abbasids in Mesopotamia, was mutilated alive and then buried in 922, after ten years of trials. Nor can one ignore the attacks launched, even today, in Egypt and elsewhere, against Ibn Arabi, another medieval mystic. The Islamic version of the Inquisition, like ours, particularly attacked the followers of its own religion, since Islam had no more escaped from fragmentation than had Christianity. The Egyptian Muslin historian Taqi al-Din al-Maqrizi (1364–1441), compiled a list of three hundred Shi'ite sects that mutually anathematized one another. More modestly, in our ownday, the Belgian Jesuit Henri Lammens has given the figure of seventy branches of Shi'ism. And is the regime of the Ayatollah Khomeini anything but the Inquisition having become the state itself?

The return to *al–Andalus* is one of the irredentist themes of the dream of Islamic imperialism to which fundamentalism has given a new intensity. One of the artful practices of the professional Muslims is, out of ignorance or calculation, to present the history of the conquest of Spain by the Arab–Berber armies as entirely beneficial to the indigenous population. In fact, the irruption of Islam into the Iberian peninsula was, for the lives of individuals and communities, rather different from the favorable reputation earned by its economic and cultural successes. Before considering Islamic Spain, which lasted from 711 to 1492, and which unconditional partisans of the Arabs have made into the golden age par excellence, let us see why this return to the past is perhaps not entirely useless for the future. Spanish diplomats knowledgeable about the Arab world have, incidentally, been recently concerned to measure the influence in Muslim public opinion of the idea of a reverse *Reconquista.* After I had alluded to this theme in an article in *Le Monde,*[3] the Spanish ambassador to Egypt rushed into my office. He wanted details and dates. I quoted a reflection prevalent among both fundamentalists and mere traditionalists: "Islam is in no hurry, but it is in its nature and its mission never to retreat definitively. Where we have once prayed facing Mecca, sooner or later we will pray again. That is the divine will."

The demographic imbalance that is in the process of becoming established around the Mediterranean in favor of its southern shore (70 million inhabitants in the south in 1950, 270 million in 2000, compared to 140 million and 200 million for the north at the same dates) can bring into the realm of the possible the notion of a return in force of Islam to Europe in the next century; a return that could be aided by local Muslim communities unless they are at least partially assimilated before then. In France alone, in 1984, these communities contained nearly three million people, and their birth rate is much higher than that of the French of European origin. Just before his death, the non–conformist Gaullist Alexandre Sanguinetti, who cannot be suspected of racism, declared: "In twenty years, taking into account both sides of the Mediterranean, there will be two North Africans for each Frenchman. Do you believe that will have no consequences? And that everyone will let us quietly live on the richest lands in the world? . . . [Our women] do not realize that if they continue [to have few children], in twenty years they will be captives of the conquerors because there will be no more men."[4] No doubt, Charles X would not have set out to conquer Algeria in 1830 if it had more than three million inhabitants.

In Marseille in 1982, a researcher from Aix–en–Provence calculated that there were 87 Muslim prayer centers, located in garages, stores and cultural centers. In the same year 16 percent of births in the city took place in North African families.[5] Representatives of the Muslim Brotherhood from the Near East, with the prestige attributed by Islam to those who come from the East, have been in the process of establishing control over these families since 1980, by claiming to possess religious "knowledge," as opposed to the French who have only "science." In the words of a blunt maxim, which provides a better basis for Muslim clericalism than any institution: "Whoever possesses religion has power over his friend."

There is obviously no question of succumbing to anti–Arab xenophobia, or writing on the walls, as has happened in Marseille: "Arab: the grave or the boat," (but I have also read: "Corsicans and Arabs into the sea"), or of proclaiming, like the Giscardian deputy Jean–Claude Gaudin in a campaign leaflet in December 1982: "A single remedy: expulsion." The North Africans belong irrevocably to the French demographic landscape, like the Italians, Spaniards, Portuguese, Poles, or Armenians. These contributions, and those of the Arabs no less than the others, renew our civilization and broaden our cultural heritage.

In autumn 1982, near the Canebière, one could see young members of the Muslim Brotherhood, apparently Egyptian, with the rough beards and white caps and "cassocks" characteristic of Islamic fundamentalists, selling to numerous North African clients, from a little open-air stand, various religious articles, and especially cassettes of sermons recorded in Near Eastern mosques and transmitting the anti–Western, anti–Communist, anti–Jewish, anti–Christian, anti–idolatrous slogans of the fundamentalist organizations. The mayor of Marseille, Gaston Defferre, although he was Mitterrand's Interior Minister, expressed his surprise: "They're already on the inside."

At the beginning of the school year in 1980, and again in 1981, an Islamic Union in France, established by Turks in 1978, especially in the Lyon region, attempted to persuade directors of public schools and social–educational centers that little Muslims "older than nine should not participate in co–educational activities, particularly swimming, sports and class outings." This dispensation was requested in a circular in the name of "cultural reasons" and "in view of the respect of legitimate regulations."

Time is short. Fundamentalist Islamic fever has shown itself not only in Marseille and Lyon. In Paris itself, members of various factions of the Muslim Brotherhood hold semi–public meetings attended by naive French people who have taken up Islam as one takes up yoga or zen. According to some sources, there are between one and two hundred thousand French citizens of European origin involved in what Father Jean Dejeux, more lucid than his colleagues, termed "ecological conversions" and what Egyptian Muslim academician Jbrahim Madkour called "birds of passage."

French political authorities are disconcerted. Often when they try to establish contact with a newly created Muslim association, they receive the reply that "since Islam has no clergy, responsibility is popular and collective, and no one in particular is qualified to be a spokesman," or else that the organization is only to "come to the aid of immigrant families abandoned by everyone else." In certain cases, the stated purpose is certainly accurate. But in how many others are fundamentalists hidden behind the mask of charity? The French government may one day be in for a nasty surprise, since it has to contend both with the "Islamic" extremism of union members close to the Communist Party and with the ambiguous game of the Algerian embassy in Paris. France, falling from one excess to another, handed over the Paris mosque in 1982 to the Algerians after having left it in the hands of a specialist of the jihad of Clochemerle: the Algerian prelate, Hamza Boubekeur. The presumptuous character in his white burnoose, a political outcast in his native land because of his "Francophile political past," and long since aligned with Guy Mollet type socialists, will have finally transformed the first Muslim institution of France into an illicit headquarters of the Algerian regime. While he did collaborate with his local partisans in 1982, his representation of Islam in France is still questionable. Although the Algerian government entered into conflict with its local fundamentalists, its utilization of Islam in France is nevertheless to be watched carefully.

It was not until January 1983 that the French premier alluded to "religious and political groups" stirring up the immigrants. At a time when his cabinet was attempting to remove the last vestiges of Christian parochialism from the school system, Pierre Mauroy, by an irony of history, was confronted with the specter of Muslim parochialism in the unions. The holy strike. In the face of this multifarious challenge, France has an enormous educational and social task to accomplish in order to incorporate the Muslim immigrants into the nation, while taking account of the fact that there will always be scant room for maneuvering between the legitimate preservation of a certain portion of original identity (religion and some cultural characteristics) and the fundamentalist temptation which, as long as frustrations persist, is in danger of being reignited by Islamic faith and ritual practices. In an asylum in Aix-en-Provence in early 1983, half the Muslim patients claimed to be Mohammed "returned to earth to restore humanity."

Let us return to the "happy society," or so we are told on all sides, of Muslim Iberia. Old Christian or Muslim chroniclers show, however, that under several caliphs, the splendors of Granada and Cordoba were accompanied by strict application of Islamic law with its attendant rigors.[6] Tarragon, Toledo, Seville, among other cities, even had their Christian communities decimated in the eighth or ninth centuries. After each revolt of non-Muslim subjects (not to mention raids on French or Italian territories not under Muslim rule), the slave markets of Spain were filled with Christians. In the middle of the ninth century, Emir Mohammed I of Cordoba decreed that the people of the Book (Jews and Christians) who did not choose the "true faith" would be separated from their wives so that they would no longer be able to father "infidels." The measure was so contrary to true Koranic prescriptions that it was never applied, but it gives an idea of the insecurity in which the non-Muslims lived at certain moments.

The history of Islamic Spain, southern France and Sicily is peppered with executions of Christians, accused by Muslim witnesses of having blasphemed against Islam, and of public sessions of payment of their special poll tax, the *jizya*, by the people of the Book, under the cries and the "legal" blows of the populace. The non-Muslims of Sicily had to wear an emblem; those of Cordoba received the order to learn Arabic;

throughout Spain, circumcision was, for a time, imposed on Christians, less in the interests of health than with the intent to harass them. And, on the French side of the Pyrenees, as elsewhere in the Islamic empire, members of the minority were forbidden to bear arms, to mount a horse, in short to be "a man," as the Muslims said. They were also obliged to inform the caliph's police of any happening, deed, or word that might harm Muslim authority. Islamic practices were sometimes even applied in Spain with a harshness unseen elsewhere; for example, when Jewish or Christian children younger than ten accidentally pronounced a Muslim formula, they were removed from their families and forcibly converted. With respect to non–Muslim adults who were merely suspected in the twelfth century of helping in the *Reconquista,* the philosopher Averroes, whose "breadth of spirit" has been celebrated for centuries, prescribed deportation without trial and, for new Muslims accused of still following Christian practices, "harsh corporal punishment."

Many trials of the period having to do with the "blood price" (*diya*) to be paid to the family of a victim by the murderer, indicate that, in the Andalusia of the caliphs, the life of a Muslim was rated double that of a Christian or a Jew, as in present day Iran. Moreover, in classic Muslim law, "the rate of the *diya,* when the victim is a free Muslim woman, is calculated on the basis of half that of a free Muslim man. The same principle of half–measure applies when the victim is a Jew or a Christian. If it is a female Jew or Christian, the *diya* will again be reduced by half."[7]

Instead of attaining equality with Muslims of Arab or Berber origin, converts to Islam were often relegated to a *sui generis* social and juridical position, contrary to the Koran, but still less discriminated against than the people of the Book. Comparison has been made between the condition of the *muwallad,* the foreigner brought up as a Muslim, that of the inhabitants of French colonies converted to Christianity. Muslim Spain experienced revolts of *muwallads* provoked by the determination of the authorities to have them continue to pay the *jizya* of the "infidels," while Koranic law imposed on the "believer" only "legal charity," the *zakat.* Finally, in Spain and elsewhere, the sometimes rather moderate zeal of the "Koranizers" toward the conquered populations and the "tolerance" toward Judaism and Christianity can be explained rather rationally by simple financial reasons, since the conversion of a neighborhood or a village would result in a substantial decrease in taxes received by the Treasury. It can also be explained by a combination of technical and religious reasons, since professions dealing with money were, and often remain, condemned by practicing Muslims, hence the need Muslim society had of followers of other religions that were less restrictive.

No one has more clearly described the complacency of the West in the face of the intellectual emptiness and the absence of contemporary original Arab–Muslim thought than Georges Henein.[8] "In this hunger for things Eastern—a veritable meal for the shabby characters who came late to the mirage of a luxury that no longer exists—there is a race to find out who will uncover the existence of a tenth–rate Arab author, who will pay tribute to obscure functionaries, to pseudo–scholars, to simple–minded and vile journalists who already take themselves for philosophers." The eagerness of an appreciable portion of the current French intellegentsia to approve without assessment or analysis everything that Islam does, says, or prescribes, even and especially if it is in a fundamentalist perspective (resembling to an extent the recent past, when the same intellectuals or their predecessors praised to the skies successively everything that came from Moscow, then Havana, Peking, and Phnom Penh), nevertheless sometimes provokes strong reactions. Thus, a specialist of the Maghrib Bruno Etienne, whose past as a supporter of Algerian nationalism allows him to speak frankly without immediately being called fascist or reactionary, burst out one day in front of an assembly of his peers: "It is extraordinary that the very people who have no words harsh enough to stigmatize the statements and theories of Monsignor Lefebvre go into ecstasy when similar statements and theories come from Muslims, with bloodshed added in."[9]

Islam, however, is too persuaded that it has possessed the "truth" for fourteen centuries to allow itself to be impressed by the sudden support of our tired intellectuals. The fundamentalists were the first to react against the new Western mania for repeating, at every opportunity, that "Islamic morality is in conformity with that of the rest of the civilized universe," that it is "compatible with socialism," and even with parliamentary democracy. From its very first issues, the Cairo magazine *al–I'tisam* ("The Refuge"), published by the dissident group for the *sharia* of the Muslim Brotherhood, issued a warning to these too good Samaritans: "We do not follow the law of the United Nations, but only that of God: the *sharia*." This is the law taken from the Koran and the Sunna (the collection of deeds and words of Mohammed) to regulate both social and religious relations.

In May 1979, during a conference of the International Association of Penal Law (headquartered in Paris) held in Syracuse, Sicily, Western jurists, particularly Americans—who were in a particularly good position because of their studies and their profession to know that the *sharia* and the *fiqh*[10] often contradict "universal" modern penal norms—wanted to caress their Muslim colleagues by promoting the adoption of a resolution asserting that "Koranic law is in harmony with the United Nations Declaration on the rights of man." The "boot–lickers" received a stinging response from a young Egyptian government official, taymur Mustafa–Kamil: [11] "We have no need of your approval. The *sharia,* the divine law, does not have to be discussed or compared to other texts, even allegedly universal resolutions. The *sharia* is the *sharia,* it is enough by itself."

On the question of whether we should constantly seek to prove that Islam is up to date, let us leave the final word to a moderate and modernist Muslim, Afaf Murad–Mahfuz, a former student in Paris, noticed for her verve by Maurice Duverger,[12] later head of the department of law and political science at the University of Helwan in Cairo. In her eyes, "Islam is, in itself, by itself, neither a factor for conservatism nor a factor for progress."[13]

Also praiseworthy is the attitude of a man like Vincent Monteil, who chose to defend Islam from within, to support its principal positions, without attempting through a fallacious presentation to make them compatible with those of his original milieu. His sincerity, his enthusiasm, his acceptance of Muslims in their particularity, his conversion to Islam (official since 1977), more earthly and political than mystical, embarrass and disturb the established categories and conformisms among the flatterers as well as the denigrators of fundamentalist Islam. He is the anti–professional Muslim, the contrary of the fashionable convert.

"To be a Muslim," for Vincent Monteil, is first of all "to place oneself apart from the superpowers. I remain French—as Charles de Gaulle said: France is my fatherland, my land and my deed—but my spiritual fatherland, as Louis Massignon told me in 1940, is the Arab world. To be a Muslim is to go to the end of myself, it is the logical conclusion of my existence."[14]

As a young Catholic, the Christian mysteries seemed to him to be "opaque" and the sacraments "useless." "Later," Monteil continues, "I became aware of two stumbling blocks between Christianity and Islam: the divinity of Jesus and the mission of the Prophet, which is only an imposture in the eyes of Christians. Any kind of syncretism seemed to me a source of confusion. On the problem of Jesus, I was never able to believe that the only God could have a son. The only rational and satisfying position seems to me that of the Koran: the Messiah, Jesus, son of Mary, is only the Apostle (*rasul*) of God. It was not until the year 325 of the Christian era at the first council of Nicea that Jesus was officially proclaimed God, [the] only son of God."

Monteil believes neither in the Trinity, nor in the Incarnation, nor in the redemption of the human race by the death of Christ. He accepts the fact that Mohammed is "the seal of the prophets." He is pleased that Islam, not recognizing original sin, does not exude that feeling of "guilt" or "remorse" after pleasure that is the "torment" of so many Christians. He is grateful that his new religion does not condemn sensuality sought for its own sake. Finally, like Massignon,[15] Monteil sees in Islam a "virile society, a simple, ascetic style of life." At most, one might criticize Monteil for taking into consideration only the physical side of Islam, at the expense of its mystical dimension.

In any event, this is far from the pallid Islam, censored and emasculated, espoused by its fashionable Parisian epigones. One cannot exaggerate the contortions Parisian intellectuals are ready to accept (even reputable intellectuals) for a visit to former colonies. Roger Garaudy, solemn as a pope, even went so far as to present a paper in Caracas on "Islam and universality in the political work of Muammar al-Qadhafi," at the Third Congress on the *Green Book* of the Libyan colonel; a pamphlet expounding the "third world-theory," based on the Koran and intended to replace capitalism and Marxism. And when it was no longer acceptable in Paris to admire the Iranian revolution, the same Garaudy described the terrifying evolution of events as "a pathetic episode of *mullahs* hungry for a power that they are incapable of exercising, and who are discrediting the Islamic revolution."[16] A durable and murderous "episode." To each his own Cambodia.

Despite, or rather because of, his fidelity to Islam, Vincent Monteil is at the opposite pole from this school of complacency, which believes it is beautifying when it disfigures. Prompt to emphasize the greatness of Islam, Monteil nonetheless does not believe himself obliged to conceal its weaknesses. Having brought out the genius of Ibn Khaldun, "a man of unequalled intuition who leapt where others crawl," he does not need, unlike others, to piously conceal the errors of the father of sociology with respect to the Blacks, "an inferior humanity, closer to stupid animals than to man," or to the Jews, charged with "concealment and trickery."

The same attitude, publicly expressed without being ostentatious, of a neo-Muslim like Vincent Monteil, which is not accompanied by an end of relations with the West (as was true for his elder, the late philosopher René Guénon, who saw particularly the spiritual aspect of Islam at expense of its daily existence), should show the way for all Europeans, whether they have become Muslims or not, who wish to serve the cause of Islam, both people and religion, by making them known and recognized in the West in their reality and not in a watered down version in conformity with our preferences. But accepting a man, a nation, or a civilization, does not mean defending their madnesses or excesses, quite the contrary. Or else, one would have to tolerate neo–Nazism in Germany, racism in the United States and elsewhere, and the Mafia in Sicily. But the professional Muslims are indifferent to these comparisons, preoccupied as they are with "selling" their specialty to curiosity seekers: an Islam without harshness or defects, a polished product proportioned according to the Western "threshold of tolerance." Chateaubriand had forged a slogan for these counterfeiters of the spirit: "Every repeated lie becomes the truth."

NOTES

1. Roger Garaudy. *Promesses de l'Islam* (Paris: Ed. LeSeuil, 1981) p. 17.
2. Currently present in Iran, Iraq and Lebanon, the Shiites have always been a minority in the Muslim world. Descended from the supporters of Ali, Mohammed's son–in–law, their doctrinal divergences from majority, and "orthodox," Sunnism do not prevent them from recognizing both the Koran and the Sunna as foundations of Islam.
3. May 18–19, 1980.
4. *Paris–Match,* October 24, 1980.
5. In Dreux, in 1982, 40 percent of births took place in immigrant families.
6. Charles–Emmanuel Dufourcq, who died in 1982, is very enlightening in this connection. See particularly *L'Espagne catalane et le Maghreb au XIIIe et XIVe siècles,* (Paris: PUF, 1966) and *La Vie quotidienne dans l'Europe médiévale sous domination arabe,* (Paris: Hachette, 1978). Most historical and religious details about Islam in Spain are derived from his work.
7. al–Qayrawani, *op. cit.*
8. Egyptian French–language writer who died in 1973. His totally unfettered spirit makes him one of the rare writers of the cen-

tury with a sharp view of both East and West, capable of making lucid and uncomplacent judgments on both. See particularly *L'Esprit frappeur*, (Paris: Encre, 1980).

9. Spoken at a roundtable on "Islam and Politics in the Maghreb" organized in June 1979 at Aix-en-Provence by the French Centre de recherches et d'études sur les sociétés méditerranéennes. It was confirmed to the author by Bruno Etienne, but it does not appear in the transcript of the roundtable. At the time, Etienne's remarks literally had the effect of a bombshell in French-speaking Orientalist circles.
10. For Jacques Berque, it is simply "jurisprudence," derived from the application of the *sharia,* while another French Orientalist, Olivier Carré, explains: "The *fiqh* is essentially practical and casuistic."
11. Taymur Mustafa-Kamil belongs to a "moderate" fundamentalist current. In 1980, at the University of Bordeaux, he defended a thesis in comparative penal law, all the more noticed because, after having noted the "abomination" of Soviet law and the "error" of French law, it emphasizes the "indubitable value" of Muslim law.
12. Maurice Duverger (1917–) is one of the most celebrated living French jurists. He has directed the theses of many students from the Third World in Paris.
13. A statement made to the author, to her Egyptian students, and during several Franco-Egyptian university functions in Cairo during the years 1978–1981.
14. *France-Pays arabes,* April–May 1978.
15. Louis Massignon was born and remained a Catholic, but he adopted the Melkite rite and became a priest of the Eastern Uniate Church (known as Greek Catholic), which unites the memory of Byzantium with present-day Arab Christendom. Massignon was married and had children, but Eastern Catholicism allows the ordination of married men.
16. *Promesses de l'Islam,* pp. 17, 44.

CHAPTER THREE

The Three Inequalities

The point of departure for the Islamic fundamentalist movement in this century was the closed society—an accurate characterization, since it has initiation rites and probationary mental and physical ordeals; it is not an anodyne "association" restricted to mutual aid and charity, though it has also been that—of the Muslim Brotherhood, founded in Ismailia, on the Suez Canal, in 1928 by an Egyptian schoolteacher endowed with rare eloquence, Hassan al–Banna, who was killed by King Farouk's police in Cairo on February 22, 1949. The seeds had been sown, and they were spread throughout the Muslim world by the martyrs Nasser created among the Brotherhood through his executions. The "congregation" has by now spread throughout the world, the West included, following Muslim immigration, losing its original unity but becoming "like salt in bread." Aside from the assassination of Anwar al–Sadat, the greatest "success" of the disciples of the Brotherhood is the Islamic revolution in Iran. In the 1950s, an obscure Iranian mullah, Nawab Safavi (later probably liquidated by the henchmen of Mohammed Reza Shah), made the Fedayin Islam—the Iranian section of of the Muslim Brotherhood—into a veritable political movement; Khomeini was one of its leaders in June 1963 when the Iranian fundamentalists attacked the imperial regime for the first time, because it was "guilty" of undertaking an agrarian reform that interfered with the interests of the Shiite hierarchy.

For more than ten years, throughout the community of Muslim peoples, from Lahore to Cairo and Fez to Jerusalem, voices have been raised, not only those of ayatollahs and shaykhs, but also those of the young, women included, of scholars, and of intellectuals trained in the West, to ask for thoroughgoing application of the *sharia*—the religious law—in Muslim countries and countries containing a Muslim population.

In Cairo, the preacher Kishk, whose more than four hundred sermons have been recorded and sell like hotcakes, not only throughout the Maghreb but in France as well, repeats, like thousands of his peers throughout the Muslim world: "The source of troubles for the Muslims lies in their abandonment of the *sharia*. We have to restore Muslim law to a place of honor for Islam to recover its former strength." And he frequently refers to the example of Iran, that has recovered its warlike vigor against Iraq, "as and to the extent that it has purely and simply reintroduced Koranic principles into its daily life and its institutions."

Abdul-Hamid Abdul-Aziz Mohammed Kishk was born in 1933 in Shubrahit, a village in the Nile delta where, in July 1798, the French army for the first time defeated the Mameluke and Arab forces, a fact not without importance even today. At the age of twelve, as his followers are fond of recalling, the future holy man already knew the entire Koran by heart. This exploit is relatively common in the Muslim world, where one can find semi–literates who are capable of only one thing, like those who memorize the telephone book: mechanically reciting the one hundred fourteen suras, starting at the end, the beginning, or the middle, on command. The child went no further because, no doubt as the result of inadequate treatment of an eye disease, he became totally blind. He was later to consider his blindness as a "divine grace, allowing me to attain a richer inner life." He was a student at al–Azhar University, to which the complete recitation of the Koran is the best introduction, and then a preacher and imam–functionary. He has been delivering his homilies in a mosque in a middle-class suburb of Cairo since 1964. His reputation began to grow after a short imprisonment in 1966 under Nasser. It reached its zenith in the summer of 1980, when a rumor circulated that Jesus Christ had appeared to him. The blind shaykh made a great deal of the importance of the return of the "Prophet" Jesus—foretold by Mohammed—at the end of time. This is one of his refrains, along with the damnation of a world "in which man gives lessons to the devil." Another imprisonment, on the orders of Sadat, in September 1981 put the final touch to a popularity that has not declined since President Mubarak has freed him and appeared to take him seriously by offering him the columns of *al–Liwa al–Islami* (The Islamic Standard), a government religious publication whose tone of bland piety almost makes one nostalgic for the outrageous but meaty fundamentalist papers banned by Sadat in 1981. Kishk accepted the offer, despite the risk of political co–optation. He has nevertheless not renounced his fundamentalist program.

In any event, the shaykh is only a poor ignorant blind man who, even so, is on occasion capable of showing a combination of finesse and humanity, not without charm for those most suspicious of him. Receiving Professor Bruno Etienne, he said: "Since you know the ideas I am defending so well, why don't you convert to Islam?" Etienne, no doubt recalling Camus's statement during the Algerian war in which he confessed that he preferred his mother to justice, retorted to the shaykh: "I don't want to hurt my mother." "That's the best answer you could have given me," concluded Kishk.

What can one say of a medical student from a "good family," a former pupil of a Franco–Arab Jesuit school in Cairo, who professes the same theories as Shaykh Kishk? Accompanied, at a respectful distance, by a young woman veiled up to her eyes, also a medical student at one of the five universities in Cairo, he declares, echoing the blind man: "Socialism and capitalism have failed among the Muslim people. We must now try the *sharia* without modification or restriction, and you will see that our renaissance will soon astound the universe."

In the neo–Louis XV salon decorated with imitation Aubusson carpets in her apartment in the outskirts of Cairo, Zaynat al-Ghazali, leader of the women's section of the Muslim Brotherhood, an educated and well-traveled woman, repeats in her own way the same refrain: "From Jerusalem to Andalusia! That is my message to Muslim mothers and women so that they will inculcate it to their children and their husbands, who will restore greatness to Islam as soon as they have reestablished the *sharia*, the entire *sharia*, in its luminous and effective simplicity!"

Believing in all innocence that he could beat the fundamentalists at their own game, Sadat held a plebiscite in 1980 to adopt Muslim law as "the fundamental source of law." The two principal wings of the *sharia*, the religious law, are the Koran, that is, "the recitation" transmitted to Mohammed in fragments from 612 to 632 by an angel from Allah, and set down in the form of 114 surats or chapters made up in all of 6,200 verses, after the death of the Prophet (in 632; the oldest existing version of the Book dates from 776), on the one hand; on the other, the Sunna or "code of conduct" containing, according to different authors, from 100,000 to 750,000 *hadiths*, deeds or sayings of Mohammed that the tradition set down in the ninth century, forty of which[1] are considered by Muslims "of indubitable importance and authenticity."

Sadat set in motion the Islamicization of existing Egyptian legislation, which was certainly in harmony with the broad principles of the Koran but, in its details, was influenced by French judicial norms. "Useless delays," clamored the fundamentalists. "Let us immediately abolish with a stroke of the pen, all present laws that are impious, and let us proclaim without further delay the reign of the holy Book!"[2]

These militant jurists seem to have no memory. The *sharia* was applied (and in any event it has always remained the ideal), throughout the Muslim world, from the earliest caliphs through the middle of the last century. It has never ceased to be the supreme law in Saudi Arabia and Yemen. In Iran, it went through a half century interruption, under the Pahlevi dynasty. In Egypt, the Levant, Mesopotamia and the Maghrib, generally only in penal matters was it gradually replaced by provisions inspired by European codes of law. This did not take place everywhere at the instigation of the colonizers, but often in response to local initiatives, as in Afghanistan, Iran, Egypt and of course Turkey, the only member of the *umma*—with the exception of Communist Albania—in which direct disestablishment of Islam was radical and intended to be complete, including the separation of religion and state. It is not for nothing that Kamal Ataturk, whom they call by his original Muslim name Mustafa Kamal, is known by contemporary Arab fundamentalists as a "traitor to Islam" and "as great an enemy of the Muslims as the Zionists." In their eyes, there is no doubt that Ataturk abolished the Caliphate in 1924 in "revenge for the refusal of Sultan Abdul-Hamid to sell Palestine to the Jews."

Present day Turkey is in few respects a showcase for the supporters (few of whom dare to show themselves) of secularization of the Muslim nations. But the Saudi Arabia of today, undermined by hypocrisy and mistrust, is hardly a better point of reference for the supporters of the fundamental law than the Egypt of the early nineteenth century or the Morocco of the early twentieth, before the "de–Koranization" of a part of their legislation.

After all, there would be no reason to criticize Muslim states that wanted to be ruled only by the *sharia* if the proposal relied on a genuine national consensus. A problem arises, however, when these countries—and this is true for a number of them—contain non–Muslim minorities who do not want to return to their former status of demi–citizens, remnants of which still survive.

Since the East has again become a matter of concern in Europe, one often hears from Westerners concerned with reducing Islamic fundamentalism to their categories, that this religion "recognizes the equality of human beings." To be honest, one would have to add: on condition that they are Muslims and that we are talking about their position before God; in that case only, *some* human beings are equal "like the teeth of a comb."

Although the Koran and the Sunna present contradictions with one another, and internally as well, the two texts are at one on the necessity, for an Islamic society worthy of the name, of respecting the fixed, unchangeable judicial supremacy of three categories of persons—men, Muslims, and masters—over three others—women, non-Muslims, and slaves. Bernard Lewis is one of therare contemporary specialists on Islam to have dared to set forth this three-fold articulation of inequality. Hence, he has been anathematized by the "true friends" of the Muslims, who accuse him of "racism" and "fanaticism."

Slavery, at least in its traditional form, is a thing of the past. Non-Muslims can leave their "inferior" status by abjuring the religion of their birth. On the other hand, Muslim women have no hope of changing sex, which would be the only means of escaping from a fate which, in the perspective of traditionalist or fundamentalist Islam, can only be named domination and segregation.

These inequalities, or substantial vestiges of them, are confirmed at every moment in the daily life of most Muslim nations, even those professing to be modern. Although the Tunisia of Habib Bourguiba had the audacity to forbid polygamy and the unilateral repudiation of wives, it has not yet risked proscribing the provision of laws in matters of inheritance that grants twice the amount to sons that is granted to daughters, a bold step that was taken by Turkey under Ataturk. The judicial uniformity on an egalitarian basis in matters of inheritance that was decreed in Kenya in 1981 provoked the wrath of the Muslim community—approximately a quarter of the population. The Minister of Justice finally conceded that its members could ask in their wills for application of Islamic law. But a Muslim adjunct minister rejected this solution, because "since the Koran is itself the will of Muslims," its provisions must also apply to an intestate Muslim. Egypt under the monarchy, although imbued with French law, never went so far as to decree that the testimony of a woman in its courts was as valid as that of a man: two statements by women are required to refute that of one man. The republic of the Egyptian "free officers" has not abolished this "anomaly" either. Less than five years after its independence, Algeria, then "the hope of all progressives around the world," forbade, through a discreet administrative circular on January 2, 1967, the marriage of a Muslim woman to a non–Muslim. A list of pettinesses created by a literal vision of the prescriptions of the Koran and the Sunna would be interminable.

Muslim husbands have the right to discipline their wives. They can repudiate them unilaterally in a few minutes, without giving any motive, and gain custody of children who have reached the age of reason (if the mother is not Muslim, custody of the children is automatically granted to the father). Jihan al–Sadat had to pester her husband for more than five years before Egyptian women were informed, in 1979, of their right to object to their husband's taking another wife; the right, if they are worthy, to custody of daughters until their marriage (previously only to the age of ten) and sons to fifteen (previously seven); and finally the right to remain in the marital home rather than being summarily thrown out on the street with her personal belongings.

All judges of *sharia* courts, in Egypt and elsewhere, are familiar with the pitiful spectacle of unfortunate women astounded to discover after the death of their spouse that they have no right to the estate because they have been repudiated several years earlier, or that they must share the inheritance with one or more co-wives.

Mrs. Sadat incurred the hatred of the majority of her male compatriots for having promoted this humanization of the status of her "sisters," which is incidentally in conformity with a modern and reasonable interpretation of the *sharia*. The students of al–Azhar, encouraged by the *ulama*, demonstrated against the "new Marie–Antoinette." Fundamentalist preachers dragged her in the mud, insinuating a liaison with President Carter. And Sadat's corpse was barely cold when voices were raised in Cairo adjuring the new *Ra'is* to abrogate the small feminist reform of 1979, "contrary to divine precepts."

The Koranic sura on women sums up rather well in a few words the unequal relations between the sexes according to Islamic doctrine:

> Men have authority over women,
> By virtue of the preference
> That God granted them over women,
> Because of the expenses they incur
> For their support. . . .
> Admonish the women whose infidelity you fear,
> Confine them in separate rooms and strike them
> But do not quarrel with them,
> If they obey you.
>
> —*Koran 4:34*

It is a universal failing to give men superiority over women. Even the most "feminine" societies retain a macho side: a Vietnamese proverb declares bluntly that "a hundred women are not worth a testicle." What makes the case of Islam more serious than others is the fact that the inferiority of women is allegedly inscribed in the will of God expressed by the *sharia*, which must remain unaltered *ad vitam aeternam*.

According to the Sunna, despite the passion he felt for women throughout his life, Mohammed did not hesitate to assert that, in a house, they were a "bad omen" and a cause of "the worst discord." Moreover, in his dream of hell, the prophet of Islam saw especially representations of female sexuality. The spirit can denigrate what the flesh desires.

We have all heard the defense of the condition of women under fundamentalist Islam. It revolves around two categories of arguments. On the one hand, unlike her Western counterpart, a Muslim women does not lose her maiden name when she marries and, even if she has a higher income than her husband, she is not obliged to contribute to household expenses. On the other, and this is the decisive argument, in his time, Mohammed considerably improved the condition of women: before him, polygamy was unrestricted, new–born girls were often buried alive, and so on. We are assured that the Revelation rectified all that.

In considering the maiden name, what does that mean in a society in which the fixed patronym is a notion recently imported from the West? The largest Arab country, Egypt (population forty–six million in 1982, or one Arab in three), has never adopted it, and the family name of each individual of either sex continues to be made up of the first names of the father and grandfather. Further, what does a wife's name mean in a system in which filiation, religion, and clan and political membership depend on the father alone? What does a maiden name mean in a society in which you can be on intimate terms with someone for thirty years without ever seeing his mother, his wife, his daughter, or his sister; without even knowing whether they exist, much less their names and origins? Arab etiquette, moreover, recommends that one refer as little as possible outside the home to female relatives. A Muslim schoolboy who had seen his mother go by was asked: "What are you looking at through the window?" "It's my house [*dar*] out walking," he replied modestly.

As for managing their resources, this is never undertaken except by older wives or widows, for, although the right certainly exists, the ignorance in which a young women is kept, and the absolute impossibility of her visiting or receiving businessmen without her husband (which would compromise the family honor), prevent her, with rare exceptions, from exercising it. As for Muslim women who work, I have questioned them from Casablanca to Beirut and from Cairo to Teheran, and I have not found a single one who knew that she could refuse to share household expenses. In contrast, not one of them —journalist, bureaucrat, doctor, nurse, or cook—was unaware that the authorization to work, to go out, to travel, derived from their husbands or fathers. Aisha Rateb, a jurist educated in Paris, was appointed Minister of Social Affairs by

Sadat, following the custom in force since Nasser of entrusting this relatively important position to a woman. She later became an ambassador. While she was a member of the government, her husband from whom she was separated, relying on his "right," one day kept a plane on the ground at the Cairo airport for a substantial period because it was about to take the government minister on an official trip abroad "without marital authorization."[3]

As for the historical argument, we are told that the Prophet imposed on the Arabs of the Hijaz, rules dealing with women that made Muslim women privileged beings in comparison to their contemporaries. Even if this were true, this status, dating from the seventh century, would perhaps benefit from some modernization. But it is not true. Mohammed was not confronted in Arabia only with uncouth nomads who treated their wives and daughters harshly. Throughout his life he had contact with authentic Christian and Jewish communities within which wives certainly had the dignity recognized by Judaism and Christianity and where little girls were not buried alive. As for polygamy, it may have been accepted by the Jews but certainly not the Christians. Mohammed, whose religious message, while possessing a solid originality, owes so much to the two other religions of the Book, could also have taken inspiration from the religious societies that he knew to establish the status of the Muslim women. He did not think this was necessary, or, some would say, he took from Christianity only the misogyny of Saint Paul and Bishop Clement of Alexandria, who preached in the second and third centuries: "All women should die of shame at the thought they were born women." But there is no basis for claiming that the founder of Islam improved the feminine condition in "a society containing only uncivilized pagans, brutalizers of women." The Muslim contribution in favor of the "second sex" appears only in contrast to the Bedouin fraction of Arab society in the seventh century. The Islamicization of certain peoples with customs particularly unfavorable for women, moreover, did not always succeed in improving their practices. In Kabylia, where women were disinherited by virtue of a Berber custom unchallenged by centuries of Islam, it was not until a French decree of March 19, 1931 (applied only after 1945), that a widow acquired inheritance rights, and then only a life interest.

On the other hand, one can argue that Muslim women were happy for centuries, ignorant as they were that a life other than perpetual solitude and suspicion could exist for the "weaker sex." This is no longer the case since education, film, television, travel, and especially foreign radio and contact with Western women have taught Muslim women that another existence, freer and more fulfilling, could be experienced.

Institutional inequality between the "true believers" (Muslims) and the others is an equally obvious fact, verified both in the texts and in practice. Two schoolboys were rolling in the dirt in the yard of a Cairo school, struggling for some marbles. A teacher, by pure chance a Christian, ran up to separate them. One of them shouted, with a furious look: "Don't touch me, I'm a Muslim!" To be a Muslim is a noble condition deserving of deference from non–Muslims. In certain distant corners of upper Egypt, a Coptic peasant will get off his donkey and move aside if he encounters a Muslim peasant on foot.

To be Muslim also means to be able to marry a Jew or a Christian and yet to be expected to refuse to allow one's brother-in-law to marry one's sister unless he converts to Islam. A non–Muslim man "is not worthy" of marrying a Muslim woman. No exception is possible, on pain of death, to this provision of the *sharia*, for centuries a source of countless romantic and family dramas in the East. To be a Muslim is also to have the right to give one's own religion to one's children, whatever the beliefs or wishes of the mother. It is to be able freely to construct a mosque, while the building of a church or a synagogue, and even mere repairs, are subject to a special administrative procedure, in fact to the discretion of the ruler. Discrimination extends even to private relations.

Here, too, the Koran is peremptory:

> O You who believe!
> Do not take Jews and Christians for friends.
> They are friends to one another.

> Whoever among you takes them as friends is one of them.
>
> —*Sura 5:51*

> May God annihiliate [Jews and Christians]!
> They are so stupid!
>
> —*Sura 9:30*

What can be, incorrectly, called the anti–Semitism of Arab–Muslim fundamentalism could fill pages and pages. In our time, it is certainly derived from the trauma provoked by the resurrection of Israel and the humiliation of the defeats in 1948 and 1967. But it also comes from the ignorance of the traditional Arab intelligentsia, incapable of distinguishing between the Israel of the Bible and that of Golda Meir and Menahem Begin; between Israelis and Jews, Judaism and the Jewish state, and so on. Naturally even more ignorant, the people, however, often show hospitality and a relative absence of prejudice toward Jews or Israelis, particularly marked in Egypt after the Camp David agreements and in Lebanon after Israel's anti–Palestinian expedition. And this was true despite an old tradition of routine anti–Judaism, expressed in a pejorative vocabulary from Morocco to Mesopotamia, Sudan and Yemen. Qadhafi shocked his co–religionists only slightly by saying, when Sadat had just been killed: "He lived as a Jew, he died as a Jew." In June 1965, in *Les Temps modernes*, an unknown Moroccan, Sa'id Ghallab, had the courage, unprecedented for a Muslim on the subject, to recount: "The worst insult that a Moroccan can make to another is to call him a Jew. My childhood friends have remained anti–Jewish. They veil their virulent anti–Semitism by asserting that the state of Israel was the creation of Western imperialism. My Communist comrades themselves have fallen into this trap. Not one issue of a Communist newspaper has denounced the anti–Semitism of the Moroccans. And a whole myth of Hitler is cultivated among the lower classes. They exalt (and delight in) the massacre of the Jews carried out by Hitler. They even believe that Hitler is not dead. And they expect his arrival to deliver the Arabs from Israel." Twenty years after this "confession," it has not been possible to find a trace of its author, perhaps because he used a pseudonym, so badly is self–criticism on this point considered by Muslim public opinion. Although the Catholic Church has confessed its sins toward the Jews (and the Muslims), fundamentalist Islam has until now remained ignorant of the notion of making amends, considering itself to be infallible.

The fundamentalist Arab press thus projects an image of the Jews sometimes worthy of the "Jew Süss" of the Nazi period. In November 1978, *Al–Da'wa*, monthly of the Egyptian Muslim Brotherhood, considered that "every Muslim who wishes to live in harmony with his faith must refuse to make agreements with Jews and to establish diplomatic, economic, and cultural ties with them, for the Jews are usurpers and aggressors. One can expect nothing from them. There can be no peace with them, only holy war. They must live as a minority within the Arab world."

In April 1980, the same publication simply set forth a list of the "twelve Jewish vices:"

1. opportunism
2. schizophrenia
3. blind racism
4. the desire to destroy the world
5. egotism
6. pillage
7. sadism
8. love of money
9. extortion
10. violation of promises
11. dishonesty
12. the art of sowing discord.

In the same year, in its October supplement for young people entitled "The Lion Cubs of Preaching," *Al–Da'wa* undertook to teach Muslim children how to recognize a Jew. Nothing was missing, not even the hooked nose, the fingernails dripping with blood or the star of David on the cloak. "O Muslim lion cub, annihilate their existence, for the Jews do not love you, you who revere God."

This anti-Jewish paranoia, which cannot unfortunately be entirely explained by Israeli intransigence toward the Palestinians, but which is obviously whipped up and expanded by that intransigence, sometimes overflows fundamentalist circles. In November 1978, the secularizing journalist Anis Mansur, a ferociously anti–Jewish confidant of Sadat, who had been thought to have reformed since he had come to know Israel and the Israelis closely, could not prevent himself from writing in the major government magazine in Cairo *October*: "The Jews, like all Asiatics, hold strong grudges. They can or will never forget. At any moment, they will unearth documents to prove that they have been persecuted. In fact, they detest all the peoples of the world."

Thus, the ritual questions that every Israeli diplomat, journalist or simple tourist asks the foreign observer on landing in Cairo are: "Do you think Sadat was sincere? Do you think peace will last without him? What does Mubarak have up his sleeve?"

Although Sadat was not of a particularly bellicose temperament, and although hispolicy of peace responded to the hope of Egypt, he obviously would not have followed this path if he had a reasonable hope in the medium term of being able to destroy Israel or at least of bringing it down to size and imposing on it the will of the Arabs.

The traditional Muslim education that the young Sadat received, emphasizing the anti–Jewish suras of the Koran, his unlimited admiration as a nationalist officer for Germany (including its Nazi aberration), the rude shock of the Arab defeat of 1948 by the Jews whom Islam had forbidden to bear arms for thirteen centuries, the confusion in Nasserite propaganda between Zionism, Judaism, and Israel are elements more than sufficient to have predisposed Sadat to be a Judeophobe as well as an Israelophobe.

In the eyes of fundamentalist Islamic activitists, the *Ra'is* "betrayed his religion and all his co–religionists by compromising with Israel and with the Christian West." He was no longer salvageable, and their aim, practically openly proclaimed in publications, tracts, speeches, and sermons, was to replace him with a "true Muslim who would restore its Islamic purity to Egypt by breaking with the Zionist entity." As long as those who profess these ideas remain a minority, even an active one provided it is outside the government, peace will not be in danger. On the other hand, if it happened that the fundamentalists took power in Cairo, it is necessary to know that the Camp David and Washington agreements have never had any more value in their eyes than the Treaty of Versailles had for Hitler. One can nevertheless imagine, especially if Israel succeeds in retaining its regional military superiority, that an Egyptian Islamic government would be satisfied with renouncing the existing treaties without thereafter launching an armed assault against the Jewish state. When this hypothesis is presented to moderate Egyptians, they express the fear that, even in the case of a simple breaking of diplomatic relations between Cairo and Jerusalem, Israel would immediately take preventive action by occupying the Sinai peninsula for the third time (after 1956 and 1967).

The *Ra'is* had long felt that the Muslim Brotherhood and their associates were the only ones who could one day seriously attempt to call his pursuit of peace into question. Thus, from the outset, he was careful to support his program with justifications from the Koran. In November 1978, he obtained from the theologians of al-Azhar a *fatwa* (ruling) in favor of peace. It was not easy, not so much because some sheikhs had to be cajoled to produce a declaration exactly contrary to the one Nasser had earlier had them pronounce to "forbid Muslims to make peace with those Jews who have despoiled the land of Palestine and committed aggression against its inhabitants," but for the simple reason that the Koran, so prodigal with justifications for war, so rich in imprecations against the Jews, treats the question of peace very scantily. A few very clear verses could nevertheless be used to defend the memory of Sadat before the great tribunal of Islam.

The sura of Mohammed ordains:

> Do not call for peace
> When you are the stronger.
>
> —*Koran 47:35*

Now, Egypt was notoriously weak in comparison to Israel when the *Ra'is* went to Jerusalem in 1977. Thus, he could make peace, if one holds to the letter of the Koran.

As for the sura of the spoils, it advises:

> If [the enemies] lean toward peace
> Do the same.
>
> —*Koran 8:61*

At this point, the defender of Sadat would have to prove, in addition, that the intentions of Israel were really peaceful when Egypt extended its hand. It would be still more difficult to get around this *hadith* from the Sunna:

> You will fight the Jews to the point that, if one of them hides behind a stone, it will say: O servant of God, there is a Jew behind me; kill him!

During his memorable voyage to Israel, before the eyes of the entire planet, the President of the Egyptian Arab Republic, at an official dinner with Prime Minister Menahem Begin at the King David Hotel in Jerusalem on November 20, 1977, wore a tie with a clear design of swastikas. The emotion, the crowd, the tears and the embraces prevented most observers from noticing this detail; the solemnity of the hour and the fear of incongruity made those who noted it keep silent. Some saw in the design on Sadat's tie a final wink, and audacious farewell to his "anti-Jewishness." It was perhaps only the work of an inept valet. In any event, there are more tangible proofs of this aberration of the *Ra'is*, the most celebrated and most irrefutable being his "letter to Hitler" published over his signature on September 18, 1953 in the Cairo government weekly *al-Musawwar*, when he was already one of the most visible figures in the Nasserite group in power in Cairo. This "missive" to the Führer had been requested of Sadat at a moment when the rumor was circulating, frequently repeated by Western news agencies, that the Nazi dictator was still alive.

> *My dear Hitler,*
>
> I congratulate you from the bottom of my heart. Even if you think you were beaten, in reality you are the victor. You succeeded in cre-

ating dissensions between the aged Churchill and his allies, the children of Satan. Germany will win, for its existence is necessary for world equilibrium. It will be reborn despite the powers of West and East. There will be no peace unless Germany becomes again what it has been. The West as well as the East will pay for this rehabilitation, whether they want to or not. The two camps will devote a good deal of money and effort with the aim of having Germany on their side, which will greatly benefit Germany, both now and in the future.

As for the past, I think that you committed some errors, like opening too many fronts and [being unable to guard against] Ribbentrop's lack of foresight in confronting expert British diplomacy. But have confidence in your country, and your people will rectify these false moves. You can be proud of having become immortal in Germany. We would not be surprised if you were to appear again or if a new Hitler were to arise in your wake.

Anwar al–Sadat

Just as he totally ignores, in this text, the millions of European Jewish martyrs of his "dear Hitler" (although he did honor their memory by a visit to their memorial in Israel in 1977), there is no record of the slightest intervention by Sadat in favor of his Jewish compatriots when, under Nasser, they were (with impunity) despoiled, humiliated, imprisoned and exiled. Moreover, he accepted as a gift from Nasser, a villa on the banks of the Nile in Cairo, which was thereafter his principal residence. It had been the home of the Castro family, Jewish merchants who had been forced into exile. Possession of this house was assured to his widow by the Egyptian parliament immediately after the assassination of October 6, 1981. As far as is known, Sadat never formulated the slightest objection under Nasser to the presence in Egypt (confirmed in 1967 in Vienna by the League of Jewish Victims of Nazism) of several Nazi criminals wanted in many European countries, who were working in anti–Israeli organs of the Egyptian administration. Among them was Luis Heiden, alias al–Hajj, author of the Arabic translation of *Mein Kampf*. Shortly before the October war of 1973, the *Ra'is* again publicly emphasized the "congenital perfidy of the Jews, recognized by the Koran."

As for Hosni Mubarak, no one is in a position to define with certainty his opinion of the Jewish state or of the Jews, but it is noteworthy that he has thus far arranged things so that he has never set foot in Israel, except once when, as vice president, he was almost forcibly brought to Beersheba for a few hours in May 1979.

In 1981, two years after the signature of the Israeli–Egyptian peace treaty, Shaykh Sharawi, a preacher whom Sadat had offered as an example for young people, used a part of his very popular religious program on television to emphasize not those statements in the Koran or the Sunna that might bring Muslims and Jews closer together, but on the contrary everything that could create conflict between them. And he added personal remarks on "the untrustworthiness of the Jews, their habit of breaking their promises," and on "infidelism, a flaw affecting anyone who does not adhere to Islamic dogma."

It must, however, be pointed out that the people of the Book—Jews and Christians—despite their status as "protected" people (*dhimmi*); despite the special tribute (*jizya*) they paid to Islamic authorities (generally suppressed in the nineteenth century, its restoration is now demanded by the Muslim Brotherhood); despite the frequent obligation they were under to wear a badge to distinguish them from Muslims, were nevertheless privileged in Muslim society in the past in comparison to "idolators" (holders of any other belief), who had a choice only between conversion and death.[4] In many mosques in Egypt, Algeria, Tunisia, and Syria (in Iran, this has already been done), every Friday there are calls for the reestablishment of the three-level pyramid—pagans, people of the Book, Islam—which, although of religious origin, nevertheless recalls other, even more sinister hierarchies. South African apartheid, regularly condemned in Near Eastern capitals also looks for justification in a religious text, the anathema pronounced by Noah against his youngest son Ham, purported ancestor of the Blacks:

> Cursed be Canaan [son of Ham];
> a slave of slaves shall he be to his brothers.

The Koran, for its part, inspired a superiority complex among Muslims:

> You make up the best community established for mankind.
>
> *Sura 3:110*

Muslim writings also suggest a preference, more esthetic than racial to be sure, for the color white, and this lent support after the death of the Prophet to certain "racial" patterns of behavior toward the Blacks.[5]

What a Biblical curse fails to make acceptable, what we fight against ourselves, should not be accepted from the Koran or the Sunna.

Islam is nevertheless not racist, since it accepts all conversions without any racial distinctions; Islam is inegalitarian on a religious basis. In 1979, the French specialist on Iran, Yann Richard, characterized "the ideological conflict between Muslim theologians and the idea of democracy" in these terms: "Equality, which is at the basis of Western ideologies, is problematic: the differences are too profound between men and women, the healthy and the ill, the educated and the ignorant, the Muslim and the non-Muslim, for it to be possible to speak of equality." In short, the *ulama* of Teheran, Mecca and Cairo could find common ground with the Parisian New Right.

This inegalitarianism is sometimes found even between Arab and non–Arab Muslims, despite the admonition of Mohammed: "Arabs have no superiority over non–Arabs, nor whites over blacks, except through piety." But a dozen other sayings of the Prophet have conferred on Arabs a *de facto* status of "chosen people," such that even today, in countries with as few Arabs as Malaysia and Indonesia, there exists an Arab snobbism in behavior and dress. "The abasement of Arabs is the abasement of Islam." "The Arabs are first among peoples." "Whoever loves the Arabs loves me; whoever hates them hates me, but only the perverse man hates them." "Whoever deceives the Arabs will not receive my intercession at the Last Judgment nor my sympathy." "Love the Arabs because the Koran is Arab, because I am an Arab, because the language of paradise is Arabic." Among Arabs themselves, the Qurayshi (member of Mohammed's tribe) is *primus inter pares*, possessing "seven unique privileges" and particular protection from Heaven: "Love the Quraysh, for whoever loves them is cherished by God." "God will harm those who have harmed the Quraysh." "Love for the Quraysh is an article of faith." "Hatred of the Quraysh is impiety." "Humanity would be colorless without the Quraysh." "Good and evil men come after good and evil Quraysh." "The worst Quraysh are better than the worst elements of other peoples." "God needs the Quraysh." I could go on.

Confronted with this excess of praise, the Persians invented *hadiths*, which they attributed to Mohammed, to counterbalance the pro–Arab bias of the Sunna: "I have more confidence in the Persians than in the Arabs." The primacy of the latter has nevertheless persisted through the centuries, although it has not gone so far as to be set down in the law.

The third *de jure* unequal relationship, which will be discussed only briefly, is that between master and slave. Nevertheless, there still exist a few residual forms of slavery or servitude in Islamic countries. Slavery was officially abolished in Saudi Arabia by Faysal II, then regent, only in 1962, and it is disappearing rather slowly. Indeed, what happens to all the poor Black Muslim pilgrims who come, sometimes on foot, from Nigeria, Niger, and Chad and never return home? They do not all die of exhaustion on arrival. In Algeria, shortly after independence, it seems that the Ben Bella government had a naive young French schoolteacher recalled to France because he had thought he was doing a good deed by pointing to cases of slavery in the Western Sahara region. Algiers probably wanted to avoid an international scandal. Ben Bella was later overthrown by Boumedienne. I do not know what became of the "serfs" of the Sahara. But in 1970, I saw their brothers in Mauritania. They were black. The owner, a young *baydani* (white) nomad, half confessed to their status, and then offered me the excuse: "Religion allows it." The right to have slaves was not "definitively" abolished in Mauritania until 1980. In August 1981, in Geneva, the group of experts on slavery of the United Nations Human Rights Commission heard Peter Davies, Secretary of the British Anti-Slavery Society, reveal that in the Mauritanian population of one million there were still at least a hundred thousand slaves bought and sold like animals, and about three hundred thousand semi-slaves and former slaves. Masters and slaves had the same religion.

Islam in fact authorizes Muslims to hold slaves, including members of their own religion. The Sura of the Cow even asserts:

> A slave who is a believer [Muslim] is worth more than a free man who is a polytheist.
>
> —*Koran 3:221*

In the nineteenth century, some Muslims, wishing to be both faithful to their religion and modern, became aware of the link in Western minds between slavery and Islam. They tried to counterattack, particularly when Cardinal Lavigerie took up the battle cry against the "Islamic slave trade." A young Egyptian, Ahmad Shafiq, with political science and law degrees from Paris, later raised to the rank of *bey* by his sovereign, recounted in a pamphlet that was republished in 1938: "On July 1, 1888, I had the opportunity to attend a lecture given by his excellency Cardinal Lavigerie in the church of Saint-Sulpice in Paris. This lecture was aimed at demonstrating to the Parisian public the horrors of slavery in Muslim countries. His Eminence attributed the odiousness of it to the religion of the Prophet. These accusations, repeated in London and Brussels, as well as in Paris, gave me the inspiration to do research on this matter in our sacred books." The excellent young man was unfortunately unable to find any condemnation of slavery there, but only "recommendations to Muslims to treat slaves with generosity and kindness" and, should the occasion arise, to "facilitate their emancipation." With total honesty, the researcher also noted "the infinitely better conditions" provided by Muslims to white slaves than to black ones.

In short, Islam disapproves of slavery but does not prohibit it; it acts in the same way for several other of its most challenged traditions, like polygamy and repudiation. It is satisfied with preaching the freeing of a slave as a means of securing Allah's forgiveness for violating a promise, unjustified repudiation, involuntary homicide (of another Muslim), or breaking the Ramadan fast. It recommends material aid to one's own slave if he wants to buy his freedom and, in the meanwhile, to treat, dress and feed him "like a brother or a companion." A female slave who is pregnant can no longer be sold or given away, and she is automatically freed if her master and father of the child should die. Nevertheless: "A free Muslim man is not put to death if he intentionally kills a slave. But the slave is put to death if he kills a free man." Similarly: "The Muslim is not put to death for the murder of an infidel, but the infidel is for the murder of a Muslim."

Muslims hardly like to be reminded of the determining role they played (along with their European accomplices) in the slave trade in sub–Saharan Africa, especially when an African head of state says of Qadhafi: "Yesterday the Arabs sold us, today they are buying us." In May 1982, President Mobutu of Zaire was not afraid of publicly attacking "Arab neo–slavery" and of characterizing Arab-African cooperation as a "snare and a booby-trap."

The uprising of the Mahdi in Sudan just a century ago can largely be explained by the opposition of Sudanese Muslims to the British decision to put an end to the slave trade, which no longer coincided with their interests and which was being vehemently stigmatized in London by the Anti-Slavery Society. A few years earlier, Maxime du Camp had described the Egyptian slave post at Asyut, between Sudan and the Golden Horn: "At five hundred paces from Syut, there is laid out a cemetery so large, that it seems to be a city next to another city. There is a profusion of dead people there, for Syut is the meeting place for caravans from Darfour. There they are released from quarantine and they seize the opportunity to mutilate their young black women and to make them fit for service in the harem."

Unlike some Europeans, present-day Arabs do not have a bad conscience about the Africans. In 1981, an Egyptian government official declared: "Islam planned the disappearance of slavery" to Western journalists who were questioning him about his attempt to justify slavery in the past in a pamphlet called *The Rights of Man in Islam.*[6] His final argument was that "the good Dr. Lebon," the traveling French doctor under the Second Empire, found that "slavery among the Muslims is better than elsewhere and that the condition of slaves in the East is much better than that of servants in Europe, for slaves in the East are part of the family." Islam would appear to have invented that rarity, the "happy" slave.

Despite the tirelessly reiterated conviction by all Arab fundamentalists that Islam will recover its grandeur only if it begins restoring the society of Mohammed's time, it is unthinkable that slavery, in the old sense of the word, will reappear in the East, if only because most of its human sources are used up and the international system is now opposed to it.

On the other hand, there is reason to be repelled by the fate reserved for the "new slaves" of the East, when one considers the ill treatment meted out to Yemenites in Saudi Arabia or to Egyptian and Tunisian peasants in Libya—all of whom are mercilessly exploited—and when one hears testimony on the miserable lot of the Palestinians in the Emirates of the Persian Gulf. Most Arab governments that import workers forbid them to bring their families and they peremptorily send them home at the end of the project or the harvest.

At the Cairo airport in April 1982, I witnessed police and customs officers insulting and brutalizing agricultural workers returning from a harvest in some Arab oil state, apparently because they didn't want to pay bribes to be allowed to bring in goods that they were legally entitled to. These officials were apparently unaware that Egyptian migrant workers bring into their country almost as much as oil does and an amount equivalent to that provided by foreign aid, the Suez Canal, and tourism combined. But no Egyptian government official has ever clearly explained this to his compatriots.

Nor has any humanitarian organization been troubled, as far as I know, by the precarious position of the "beasts of burden" that Muslim migrant workers often become in the Arab world, and sometimes even in their own countries. They are the most miserable of landless peasants.

Here as well, too strict an adherence to the literal meaning of the texts has led Islam into lamentable errors. Contempt for peasants is not unique to Muslim countries, but among them it can rely on a statement attributed to Mohammed by the Sunna:

> This [a plowshare] will not enter a family's home unless God also causes degradation to enter as well.

The class prejudices of Mecca merchants (the class to which the Prophet belonged, as did his first wife, the rich widow Khadija) are still visible today in Islamic societies. They have not driven the "merchants from the temple," but have on the contrary made them the leaders of the city. Reverence is paid equally to the warrior and the caravan driver; roles that Mohammed himself played. On the other hand, these societies turn their backs on writers, since the Prophet had fierce quarrels with poets. In this other level of inequality (in contrast to those of women, religious minorities and slaves) that is not inscribed in the law, the peasant, the one who touches the earth with his hands, and not the "noble shepherd," occupies the base of the social triangle. A Nubian proverb bluntly sums up the situation: "It is better to be sexually assaulted than to cultivate the land."

NOTES

1. Imam Nawawi, *Quarante Hadiths* (Tunis: Sud–Editions, 1980) (bilingual edition).

2. In the years from 1977 to 1981, this kind of statement returned like a leitmotif in the speech and writing of Egyptian fundamentalists: sermons in mosques, publications, interventions in parliament, conversations and so on. It perfectly mirrors the climate of the period.
3. Author's personal documentation. This incident is alluded to in *Le Monde*, June 6–7, 1976.
4. To be complete, we should add to the religions benefiting from the "protection" due from Islam: the Sabeans (also known as Mandeans or Christians of Saint John the Baptist), a syncretistic sect now reduced to a few tens of thousands of people living a rather scorned existence in Iraq and Iran. The Sabeans integrated into their doctrine certain elements of Persian Mazdeism (Zoroastrianism), but they remained distinct from that religion. Persian Zoroastrians and Hindus in the Mogul empire were more or less *de facto* assimilated to the people of the Book.
5. Bernard Lewis, *Race and Color in Islam* (New York: Harper & Row, 1971).
6. Cairo: Minbaral–Islam, (1981). (Trilingual edition, Arabic, French and English.)

CHAPTER FOUR

Cows in a Meadow

As we have seen, the question of a return to the totality of Islamic law has not arisen in Saudi Arabia or Yemen, where the Koran has always been the only law and even the only Constitution. On the other hand, this reintegration of juridical and religious realms has taken place in Pakistan, Iran, and Libya, and was in preparation in Egypt until the assassination of Sadat; thereafter, Egypt has remained uncertain on the question. With respect to women and non–Muslim minorities, when those minorities exist, the restoration of the absolute power of the *sharia* immediately raises a simple problem of human rights.

When the General Assembly of the United Nations adopted the Universal Declaration of Human Rights on December 10, 1948, the Soviet Union and other communist states, the Union of South Africa, and Saudi Arabia were candid enough to abstain. The representative of the Imam of Yemen preferred not to attend. Among the member countries then capable of applying the *sharia,* Afghanistan, Egypt, Iraq, Lebanon, Pakistan, and Syria voted for the resolution, and they have not officially repudited that decision.

Reinforced by other resolutions in 1966 and 1976, the Universal Declaration still has only symbolic value, but it enjoys enormous prestige. All communist regimes, along with a series of "Christian" dictators of the Third World (and only yesterday of Western Europe), are unconcerned; they are rivals in the attack on human rights. Condemnations and protests may proliferate from every direction; the results are slender, although preserving a single life or single freedom from arbitrary force is never an empty victory. But we must be logical: the struggle for human rights, at least as long as the international community continues to define them according to the Declaration, also has to be brought wherever Islamic law is literally applied. In this respect, it is not surprising that the United Nations Human Rights Commission's twenty-year old program directed toward "the elimination of all forms of intolerance and discrimination based on religion or belief" has remained moribund, despite the attempt to revive it in April 1981. Where is the state, with Islam as its official religion, that would now dare to sign a document authorizing the propagation of all beliefs, and possibly the eventual conversion of Muslims to other creeds?

The Universal Declaration proclaims the "equal rights of human beings," prohibits distinctions based on sex or religion, recognizes the right to marriage by mutual consent of the partners without obstacles of a religious nature, provides for the freedom to change one's religion, the right of any peson to take part in the public affairs of his country, and so on. With reference to the last principle, an Iraqi jurist correctly pointed out, with some amusement, that Great Britain, a model of democracy, was in violation of the principle because the sovereign can only be a member of the Anglican Church, while the kingdom includes a large number of other religious communities, particularly Catholic.

Wherever the *sharia* is applied, the Declaration of Human Rights is no longer respected, as far as religious minorities and women are concerned, and generally with reference to religious freedom.

In order to outflank such criticism, a certain "Islamic Council for Europe," created in London in 1973 and given a mandate by several "Muslim organizations" reportedly funded by Pakistan, Saudi Arabia, Libya and other Muslim countries, met in Paris in 1981 to proclaim the "Islamic Universal Declaration of Human Rights." After all, why not? Paris has its "Club for Socialist Human Rights." But while the latter would like to broaden the U.N.'s Universal Declaration, the Islamic document is restrictive, since all the rights that it proclaims are valid only if they conform with the *sharia.* A Palestinian, Sami al-Dib Abu Sahlieh, head of the Arab-Islamic department of the Swiss Institute of Comparative Law has, moreover noted differences between French and English translations and the Arabic version of the Islamic declaration, with the latter being probative.

"Except as provided by Law,[1] every individual in the community has the right to public office," says the translated document, while the Arabic text explains "without distinctions based on race or class." It obviously does not add "based on sex or religion," since the *sharia* has established a distinction, principally in terms of power, between men and women, Muslims and non-Muslims. It is Islamic dogma that every Muslim should be ruled by a male co-religionist. The Mameluke Queen Shagar al-Durr of Egypt, who held Saint Louis (King Louis IX) prisoner and who was killed by blows from bath clogs, and the more fortunate Queen Aruwa of Yemen, who seems to have died in her bed—both of whom were certainly Muslims—have been cited by Koranic jurists, because of their sex, as typical examples of infringement of the *sharia.* "A country ruled by a woman is heading for destruction," says the Sunna. Léopold Sédar Senghor, because he was Catholic, caused much irritation in Senegal while he was president, since the country was 85 percent Muslim; similar irritation has been provoked in Lebanon by the fact that the President, since the end of the French mandate, has always been a Christian. In 1977, a Shi'ite officer of the regular Lebanese army told me, as he sipped a glass of arak at a sidewalk cafe in Tyre, "I have nothing against the good president Sarkis, but what do you expect, we Muslims can never get used to the idea of seeing a Christian at the head of our country." And this was before the Islamic revolution in Iran, which has provoked a radical upsurge in the Lebanese Shi'i community. After the Iranian earthquake, Nayla Subra, westernized heir of a great Beirut Shi'i family and daughter of an ambassador, said to me: "The truth is now in Teheran." "How can you say that when you're wearing a fashionable dress and drinking a glass of Bordeaux? You would be the first victim of an Islamic regime." "But you don't understand anything. I am lost for them. It's for the others." And tears came to her eyes.

In September 1975, when Christian fighters in Beirut and the mountains seemed on the point of succumbing to the Palestinian offensive, Husayn al-Quwwatli, one of the principal leaders of the Lebanese Dar al-Iftah, a Sunnite institution that produced *fatwas,* thought that the time for a "religious" government of the country was approaching—since all Arab countries had more or less Islamic political systems, it would be appropriate to describe Lebanon as a pluralist state, since leadership was shared among communities—and recalled that a Muslim could be governed only by a brother in Islam. Questioned about this *faux pas* on Lebanese television in January 1981, when Christian positions on the front were less precarious, Quwwatli, eyes lowered, merely murmured: "If what you understood has wounded you, that wound affects me as well." He was exquisitely polite, but was careful not to contradict his 1975 statements. Even if he had wanted to, he could not have done so, and this will remain the case as long as an attempt at a new interpretation of the *sharia,* as at the dawn of Islam, has not reappeared among Muslim jurists.

Innovation was certainly not on the agenda of those who composed the "Islamic Declaration of Human Rights," a fashionable costume woven out of old cloth. Thus, the document does not explicitly mention the right to change one's religion, for good reason, since the *sharia* does not give Muslims that right. Similarly, the right to marry is recognized in "the Muslim framework" only "in conformity with the religion, tradition, and culture" of the bride or groom, which gives off an odor of the ghetto. "Human rights are a human invention, while Islamic precepts are of divine origin and thus have primacy," declared, in 1978, a year before his death, the great imam of Egypt, Abd al-Halim Mahmud, shaykh of al–Azhar, and former student of the Sorbonne.

The most comic thing, if one can call it comic, is that the pan–Muslim organization of London placed Ahmad Ben Bella, former head of state of Algeria who has "infinite respect"[2] for the Swiss Nazi banker François Geroud, in charge of international promotion of "Muslim human rights." This was the same Ben Bella who, despite appeals from all sides, had repopulated Algerian prisons with political prisoners of "right" and "left," and had allowed the police and army to restore the "scientific" torture that the French, themselves pupils of the Nazis (thus peoples transmit horror to one another), had introduced.

At a meeting of the central committee of the National Liberation Front, the party in power, men like Harbi raised the question of the harsh treatment given to Kabyle dissidents by government troops, but Colonel Hawari Boumedienne, who was to overthrow Ben Bella in 1965, then Minister of Defense, gave the answer that General Massu had given during the Algerian war: "If you have another way to make the rebels talk . . .," and Ben Bella caved in. Ben Bella also rejected appeals to abolish the death penalty, trumping in advance the *ulama* of Saudi Arabia for whom such an abolition would be "insulting for God." Ben Bella permitted the execution of former colleagues and of young hotheads, who were called "counterrevolutionaries." Ben Bella propounded economic measures whose catastrophic consequences can still be felt in his country's agriculture. Their only purpose was to force into exile the few hundred Algerian farmers who had the "misfortune" to be of European ancestry. Ben Bella, finally, could have done so much, by relying on the enormous prestige of Algeria at the conclusion of its war of independence (1954–1962), to shake up, modernize, and change the Arab–Islamic world, but in the end he was, once in power, nothing but an autocrat, merely a bit more pretentious than his peers.

Despite the restrictions on human rights implied by the application of Islamic norms, it has rarely been possible in the last few years to open a book or listen to a lecture on Islam without encountering emphasis on the "tolerance" of Islam, particularly in religious matters, contrasting, according to most writers, with Christian anti–Semitism or the intolerance of Catholic Spain toward the Muslims after the *Reconquista.* It is now rare for a Muslim head of state, politician, or intellectual to speak of Islam without trotting out a statement about the "tolerance" of Muslim doctrine.

For a time, I was taken in by this idyllic picture. My eyes were opened by letters from Arabized Christian readers, particularly from Coptic students in France, that I received after having written of this celebrated Islamic tolerance.[3] "We do not want to be tolerated in a country where we were at home, where we were Christians for several centuries before the Muslim invasions; we want equal rights with our Muslim compatriots."

Tolerance could be the charity of the intelligentsia. It is at bottom most of the time only a favor granted by the stronger, that can be called into question whenever its dispenser decides to do so. It is never a right. To tolerate is to refrain from prohibiting when one might, and this is sometimes painfully clear; it is in the end a sword of Damocles, while minorities constantly hope for respect and equality.

In religious matters, the reputation for tolerance of Islamic doctrine is totally unfounded. In fact, it must be admitted that the first virtue of tolerance is to accept that those who hold any particular faith may leave it whenever they choose. Now, the *sharia* is very clear on the question: "If a man changes his religion, kill him." The classic doctrine of orthodox Malikite Islam, in force particularly in North Africa, even provides: "A man who abstains from prayer, denying the legitimacy of that institution, is identical to an apostate; he will be asked to repent for three days, and if he does not make an act of contrition, he will be put to death." "Changing religion" must be understood as "leaving Islam," for the conversion of any non–Muslim to the faith is on the contrary a benefit, a festival, and a humiliation for those who remain "unbelievers." In the villages of Upper Egypt, the postulant is promenaded among the population amid cries of "he has embraced the true religion." The Copts take refuge at home. Nasser prohibited these troubling demonstrations. But who is to control what happens in distant villages of the Nile valley? In Persia before the Pahlavis, any minority individual who joined Islam automatically took over ownership of all his family's goods. Khomeini is said to have revived the custom.

Examples of "ordinary intolerance" are not hard to find in the daily life of most contemporary Islamic peoples. From the time of Bilal, the Abyssinian slave of Abu Bakr, one of the fathers-in-law of Mohammed, who made Bilal the first muezzin of Islam, prayer has been begun by a human voice from the top of a minaret. The muezzin was a "living bell," in the phrase of Edmond About. His threnody, lost in the uproar of daily activity or swallowed up by the dark, was scarcely caught with attentive ears by any but the faithful. The only detail of concern to the community was that the muezzin not have too keen eyesight—the ideal would be that he be blind—so that women without veils, carrying out their household tasks on roofs and in courtyards did not have to take refuge at the time of the *adhan*—the invitation to prayer.

In the age of electricity and especially with the introduction of the tape recorder and the loudspeaker, the stairways of minarets have become dusty and the muezzin has become something like a disk jocky in a night club. There are no longer any Koranic chants worthy of the name, throughout Islamic territory, except for Cairo, where idolized muezzins like shaykh Abd al-Basit have made fortunes from their voices. At the beginning, only the largest mosques, often located in open spaces at a substantial distance from residential areas, could afford stereophonic equipment. Today, in large cities and small villages, the most modest sanctuary has its loudspeaker which, five times a day, turned to full volume and often distorted, vibrates through the atmosphere. This is fine for daylight hours, or even during the siesta, but at four in the morning, the call to prayer of *fajr* (dawn), which few Muslims observe, now brutally awakens millions of people throughout the Islamic world. Children cry, adults get up for a drink of water or to urinate, dogs bark, and patients call for nurses in hospitals, for they too have their own mosques. The recorded voice continues relentlessly: "Ya mu'min! (O believer), Ya muslim! (O Muslim), prayer is better than sleep!"

With entire Muslim countries suffering from disturbed sleep, a few people have had the audacity to ask the rulers to enforce municipal noise regulations. But, just as the mayor of Paris does not dare to take on the Parisians whose dogs soil the sidewalks or those who violate the 1975 language law by Americanizing their signs, no Arab municipality has had the courage to order the early morning "hypocrites" to turn down the sound. The authorities are also absent whenever some fundamentalist makes trouble for Eastern Christians who ring the bells of their churches at ten in the morning on a day of celebration; those bells are one of the "victories" of the minority from the last century which Muslim extremists now want to take away from them.

In villages or mixed neighborhoods in Egypt where Copts clearly outnumber Muslims, fundamentalists have rented apartments from which they broadcast, night and day, recorded readings from the Koran. Obviously, many Muslims also suffer from this aural pollution that does not respect religious distinctions (and is certainly not perceptible in the palatial hotels on the banks of the Nile where visiting professional Muslims are housed), but, aware of the immediate response they would receive from their activist co–religionists ("Shut up, the faint–hearted are even worse than renegades"), they prefer to remain silent.

In September 1981, to distract public opinion after the harsh religious conflicts in Cairo, the Egyptian government press, in this case in harmony with the fundamentalists, gave great play to the police discovery of a Coptic troublemaker, a lecturer in an agricultural school who had been sending anonymous letters to Muslim dignitaries since 1979. The press was close to making him responsible for the tension between religious communities. One of these letters, published in the daily *al–Ahram,* proclaimed: "Islam is the religion of uproar and of forced awakening in the middle of the night, of loudspeakers and drumbeaters." Fuad Girgis, the author of these lines and others of the same kind, was simply a *kafir* (unbeliever), whose house had been the target of nerve–wracking broadcasts of odes from the Koran produced every night by the local fundamentalist group. Unable to protest, having lost sleep and half his reason, the unfortunate man relieved himself with inflammatory letters. It may be that the cell in which he may still be imprisoned looks out on the minaret of the penitentiary. Sadat, who lived for most of the year in a property without a muezzin, on the Nile delta, twenty–five miles from the tumult of the capital and sheltered by large trees, had adopted a policy patterned after that of Mazarin. "Let them sing, as long as they pay," said Mazarin in response to the satirical attacks made on him, while Sadat thought: "Let them declaim the Koran all day long provided they keep quiet." The result was that the Egyptians suffered from insomnia, and the Ra'is was the victim of young men stirred up by interminable tirades from the Koran. After the crime of October 6, 1981, the noisy mosques were quiet and withdrawn. Once the storm had passed, six months later, they had returned even more loudly to their apostolic uproar.

Another example of the fundamentalists' lack of respect for opinions different from theirs was the affair of Franco Zeffirelli's film of the Christ story. After a few years of hesitation, the film was finally shown in Egypt, with enormous success. The Muslim Brotherhood had no objection to the first episode, which contained nothing really contrary to Islamic Christological doctrine. But the second episode created an uproar—it showed the crucifixion. This is denied by the Koran, "since the Envoy of Heaven could not have suffered a slave's punishment." So leaflets were distributed before the showing of the second episode, threatening arson of the theaters if this "insult to divine revelation" were shown. Sadat could have guarded the theaters, since thousands of citizens of every faith wanted to see the second episode of the film. He preferred to give in to the fundamentalists; Zeffirelli's film, of course without explanation, was withdrawn from exhibition. In 1980, the rector of the University of Cairo similarly retreated in the face of threats from fundamentalist student groups, who had sworn to "blow everything up" if the Egyptian filmmaker Yusuf Shahin's *Alexandrie, pourquoi?*, which presents Jews and Christians (as well as Muslims) in a favorable light, was shown on university grounds.

And what of the fantastic, never-ending question of alcoholic beverages? An entire book could be written on the theme, with all its dramatic and ridiculous episodes. Early in the colonization of Algeria, a Frenchman noted that the only difference between a French peasant and a *fellah* was that the latter never came home drunk. He correctly attributed this benefit to Islam. Today, the intermixture of populations and the commercial permeability of borders makes the effective prohibition of alcohol in any given territory impossible. There is a plentiful supply of alcohol in Saudi Arabia because of the desert frontier with Jordan and the resourcefulness of foreign airline personnel. And in Kuwait, at the risk of imprisonment, whiskey is served in teapots. The United States is not the only country where prohibition has stimulated thirst.

In the mental confusion that seized Egypt toward the end of Sadat's reign, when no one knew, not even the government itself, whether the government was leaning toward modernization or toward obscurantism, the debate on alcohol took on an increasingly grotesque character. During Ramadan, whoever might be Muslim was refused beer or wine even in the restaurants of the grand hotels of Cairo. Furthermore, in certain establishments, the rule was applied to Egyptian Christians but not to foreign Muslims. The governors of Port Said and Suez, following small fundamentalist demonstrations, prohibited alcohol in their cities, even though they are international ports. This provoked crowds in Ismailia, the third city on the banks of the canal, whose governor chose not to imitate his colleagues. The most "comic" episodes occurred on Egyptian planes leaving Cairo International Airport where, with airplane engines running, startled tourists witnessed "dry" stewardesses confronting "wet" stewardesses trying to prevent them from offering Egyptian wine to the passengers. There was even a prohibitionist pilot who ordered the flight personnel to return the alcohol it had brought on board for refreshments and duty-free sales: "We cannot carry the Koran and wine in the same plane." To please fundamentalist travelers, a copy of the holy book had been put on display in every airplane of the Egyptian company. The newspapers seized on these incidents; the shaykh of al-Azhar supported the "drys." Asked to decide for the "wets," Sadat was careful not to. Finally, there were flights with wine and others without, following the convictions of the pilot, who was after all the captain of the ship.[4]

I am so little a drinker that when I worked for *Le Monde* in Algiers, and later in Cairo, there were rumors in some foreign embassies that I had converted to Islam. Nevertheless, I once wrote an article expressing the wish that Muslims would relax about the problem of alcohol, like the indulgent imam Abu Hanifa, the eminent Arab-speaking Persian jurist of the early days of Islam, who declared at the court of the first Abbasid caliphs of Baghdad that alcohol was, if not licit, at least "tolerable."[5] I could also have referred to the contemporary Egyptian shaykh, Mohammed Sa'd Galal, a respectable professor of theology at al-Azhar, who had authorized Muslims to drink beer; he had to take refuge at home to avoid being mobbed by young fundamentalist militants who had given him the nickname "Shaykh Sa'd Stella" alluding to a popular brand of beer.

The mere reference to the indulgent imam of the eighth century produced an avalanche of letters to *Le Monde,* ranging from trivial insults to learned dispute. Our most distinguished correspondent was the head of the publishing company Editions du Seuil, Michel Chodkiewicz, who had converted to Islam as an adolescent, had taught in Algeria, was a skilled translator of the Emir Abd al-Qadir, and was highly knowledgeable about Islam. He wrote to the the editor of *Le Monde,* Jacques Fauvet: "I would be curious to know how the act of making the use of wine licit for Muslims would contribute to the progress that M. Péroncel-Hugoz calls for. I did not know that the rate of alcoholism was an adequate measure of the degree of civilization of human societies."

Jacques Fauvet, both amused and embarrassed, asked me to answer the scrupulous publisher. I wrote in particular: "To return to this dispensation of Hanafism[6] [on alcohol], and generally to respect for the Koran's spirit of leniency, would not, of course, resolve all the problems of contemporary Islamic societies, but it would perhaps allow the avoidance of certain excesses, beginning with alcoholism, which is known to increase whenever there is prohibition."

Michel Chodkiewicz answered me, directly this time: "As far as wine is concerned, it is formally prohibited in the Koran and the Sunna . . . the only divergence [among the four great orthodox juridical schools] having to do with applicable penalties . . . . Abu Hanifa and his disciples take a position that is less strict than the three other rites only with respect to *nabidh,* a drink made by steeping grapes or dates in water for a few hours. And even so, it was generally used only by the sick and in small quantities (the Prophet himself sometimes drank *nabidh,* but threw it away when it was more than three days old). Starting from that point, certain modernist Muslim jurists have tried to assimilate various alcoholic (more or less) drinks to *habidh,* including beer and cider (never wine, as far as I know). This assimilation is chemically absurd and legally indefensible."

I immediately replied with the story of the old Turkish–Egyptian princess,[7] a very good Muslim, who had promised a large reward to the jurist who would demonstrate to her that alcohol is really prohibited by the Koran, "and who died leaving her money to the poor." I added, in conclusion: "Doesn't the Koran say, moreover, that the believers will find wine in paradise? As Omar Khayyam sang, why prevent those who want to taste the beatitudes now from drinking a little wine in their lifetime?"

Often, when Islam is presented as an example of tolerance, I think, with no need to refer to fundamentalism, of the case of Mecca. Of course, when one has seen the Holy Sepulcher in Jerusalem transformed into "Disneyland" by groups of American tourists, one can only inwardly approve of the Muslims for having forbidden their holy places of Mecca and Medina to non–Muslims. Even so, when the police suddenly stop you on the road from Jidda to Mecca to verify your religion on your visa, and when you see large billboards forbidding "non–Muslims" to go any further, you feel seized by mixed feelings, among which humiliation finally dominates. "You are not worthy to enter on this sacred land." This is what you conclude the exclusion means, as you take mountain roads skirting Mecca. And you begin to imagine the international protests that would arise from every direction if the Catholic Church or Israel were to close off some sanctuary or holy place to the followers of other religions. I have never heard even a timid voice protest against the exclusion of non–Muslims from Mecca and Medina. Does that mean that a clear act of intolerance, of rejection of the other, has to be accepted if it is several hundred years old?

Here is another example, political this time, of a certain form of Islam, unfriendly to non–Muslims, but which on this occasion provoked the reaction it deserved within the *umma* itself. In 1972, a delegation of the Ba'th party, in power in Damascus, was sent to Tripoli by General Hafiz al–Asad, Syrian head of state, in connection with the activities of the ephemeral Federation of Arab Republics. This delegation was led by a Christian—one of the rare advantages of the Ba'th dictatorship in Damascus is a tendency toward secularism, which is expressed in a certain effort not to discriminate against the local Christian minorities. Qadhafi abruptly let it be known, by a message from the control tower, that "only Muslim passengers could land." There was hesitation and negotiations on board. Informed in Damascus, Asad ordered his delegation to take off again immediately for Syria. Kamal Nasir, a Palestinian Christian and spokesman for the P.L.O., who was assassinated by Israeli commandos in Beirut in 1973, had had a similar misadventure in Libya.

The master of Tripoli thinks that it is "aberrant" to be an Arab and a Christian at the same time. "If Christian Arabs are authentic Arabs, they must embrace the Muslim faith," thundered Qadhafi in August 1980. Although he challenges the right of Lebanese Christians to live in a state where they speak as equals to their Muslim compatriots, Qadhafi, on the other hand, has conceded to the Armenians the right to establish their own country, on Soviet territory, to be sure. If Armenian national demands develop, it will be interesting to see what attitude Muslim governments will adopt, since an Armenian state would necessarily take part of its territory from Turkey, a member of the Islamic *umma.*

The fact that Christian Europe has for centuries presented the spectacle of the most hideous intolerance—as much toward certain "deviant" Christians as toward the Muslims of reconquered Spain or the Jews (the latest and most terrible spasm of anti-Semitism of a western nation being the genocide committed by a Germany that was Nazi, of course, but also Christian)—obviously throws a good light on the less hypothetical survival during the same period of Jewish and Christian minorities under Islamic rule. While French Algeria in the forties "sent its Jews back to their workshops," according to the "witticism" of General Giraud, ephemeral co-president with DeGaulle of the French Committee for National Liberation, Sultan Mohammed V of Morocco refused to have his Jewish subjects wear the yellow star. But if, as former president Ben Bella (now a representative of a certain Islamic fundamentalism with a respectable face) proclaims, the peoples of Christian civilization should experience a collective sense of guilt because of Hitler's anti-Semitic persecutions, there is no reason why the Muslim community as a whole should not be declared collectively responsible for the Armenian genocide perpetrated in 1894–96 and 1915–18 under the banner of the Caliph of Islam himself.

It is legitimate to compare current events with historical parallels. It is, on the other hand, questionable to attempt to justify injustices or crimes committed now, in the name of a government or a people, by recalling equivalent or worse actions carried out by another system or another nation in the past. In response to a journalist on the Europe 1 radio station, who found it difficult in September 1981 to imagine "the coexistence of the idea of human rights with that if Islam, in view of Islamic history and daily life in Iran," Ben Bella asserted: "Nowhere has blood flowed more freely than in Europe. During the Second World War, sixty-two million people[8] were killed, liquidated, including six million Jews. You secreted Nazism, fascism, and now the gulag, that's a lot of blood."

None of the eighteen French journalists who were there had the presence of mind or enough historical knowledge to answer Ben Bella that if Europe had collective responsibility for the atrocities of German Nazism or Russian Stalinism, there was nothing to prevent declaring Islam, as a whole, guilty, not only for the elimination of a million and a half Armenians, but also for the massacres of Jews carried out in Arabia in the age of the Prophet, for the expulsion of all non–Muslims from the region decreed by Caliph Omar ibn al–Khattab,[9] for the anti–Christian persecutions of Caliph al-Hakim in Egypt and Palestine at the beginning of the second millennium of the Christian era, or for the persecution of Maronite Christians by the Druze in Lebanon in 1860, not to mention Syrian or Palestinian bombardments of Christian civilians in Beirut and Zahle between 1975 and 1982.

A certain degree of complicity and a few magnificent gestures are not enough to obscure the reality of the fate of non–Muslim communities of the *umma* during the centuries of "Islamic tolerance." The real content of the status of "protected" minorities was too often made up of perpetual insecurity, extortion and contempt.

Although the West's prejudices, hostility and calumnies against Islam have been less tragic than anti–Semitism, strictly speaking, they are nevertheless unjustifiable. But there is some explanation for these attitudes. The Christians of the Middle Ages had restored "the immemorial unity of the old middle sea of the Ancients." The Muslim invasions destroyed that unity, cast fear throughout Europe, and proposed a new faith that scandalously claimed that belief in Christ was outdated. According to the great Belgian historian, Henri Pirenne, the shock was so great that, in a protective reflex, it gave birth to

European feudalism with all its associated psychological characteristics.

The difference between the way Muslims treated Christians and Christians treated Muslims in the Middle Ages can thus be explained by the fact that the Prophet's horsemen arrived as invaders in Christian lands over which they had no rights and where they needed the collaboration of local populations, while the knights of the Cross were retaking possession—particularly with the *Reconquista*—of land that had been seized from their ancestors, explaining their revengeful spirit. The status of protection—subjection or *dhimma,* which is, or would today, be nothing but a stopgap for minorities in the Islamic world, represented, in unsettled periods, a certain juridical guarantee of the survival of non-Muslims.

Since then, the West has evolved. It has expressed, often very sincerely, its recognition of guilt. It seems, at least in part, to have undergone profound reforms, and it is constantly struggling, through law and the support of a significant segment of public opinion, to prevent the return of the old demons. Above all, the West does not have, and has never had, a supreme law "dictated by God," as the Muslims do, and thus no settled course of conduct toward non-Christians. Islam has generally been less harsh toward its minorities, but it has not changed: a superior law has imposed an attitude toward those minorities whose settled injustice is claimed to be immutable.

The agreeable impression of tolerance, cordiality, and familiarity that one often feels in daily intercourse with Arabs is finally based more on nonchalance, indifference, and laxity than on genuine acceptance of the other, the non-Muslim. The characteristic social grace of the East increases the illusions of the Westerner. Their simple habits and indulgent attitudes are in fact based on an invisible foundation (extremely complex and rigid) of traditions and obligations that make themselves felt whenever religion or the "honor" of the family is at stake; attitudes that social pressure prevents them from changing. "Islamic tolerance is like cows in a meadow; they can go everywhere, but not beyond the fence; if they try to go through it, they get an electric shock," concluded a European

Dominican after having observed Muslims sympathetically for thirty years and translated their theological texts into French. The comparison, of course, applies to those who are outside the enclosure.

It should also be noted that the East is always more open and flexible for a foreign Christian than for a local one. This is deceptive, and often makes a Westerner think that his local co–religionists benefit from the same attitude on the part of the Muslims. The case of the Copts of enigmatic Christian Egypt presents itself as a thousand-year chronicle, still in progress, of Islamic–Christian relations in a situation of Muslim supremacy.

NOTES

1. The capital letter in translation, since in Arabic all letters are lower case, is intended to indicate that what is being referred to is Koranic law, the *sharia*.
2. *La Tribune de Lausanne,* June 19, 1982.
3. *Le Monde,* November 26, 1977.
4. In 1984, alcohol was definitively prohibited on Egyptian airlines.
5. *Le Monde,* October 8, 1981.
6. The juridical school (or rite) of Abu Hanifa, whose principal characteristics are still recognized by the Muslims of Turkey, India, and China.
7. Emineh Halim, granddaughter of Mohammed Ali, founder of modern Egypt.
8. The more "reasonable" figure of thirty–eight million dead, including civilian victims, is generally accepted by historians of the war years.
9. The Caliph's decision was even more iniquitous than the expulsion of Muslims from Spain in the sixteenth century; after all, their ancestors had come as conquerors—exactly like the *pieds–noirs* in Algeria, whose descendants also had to leave their native land—while the Jews and Christians of Western Arabia, with whom Mohammed himself had established coexistence agreements, had settled in the peninsula several centuries before the establishment of Islam.

CHAPTER FIVE

The Coptic Enigma

In the Arab East, which is in many respects very hospitable and indulgent, there are two taboo subjects that a foreigner would be well advised not to address if he does not want to incur general disfavor: the status of women, of course; and, less well known, the fate of religious minorities, in the past Jews and Christians, now only Christians, with the exception of four thousand Jews still "held" in Syria.

Although Muslims do not lack arguments—from ancient practices derived from the prescriptions of the Koran and the Sunna—to justify, in their own eyes, their treatment of women and non-Muslims, they are embarrassed when confronted with the egalitarian ideals generally accepted, if not always respected, in the contemporary non–Islamic world. The reactions of Muslims, fundamentalist or not, aimed at defusing questions or criticisms from Westerners about their treatment of Christian minorities, express as much embarrassment and bad conscience as they do the discontent of a community whose conviction that it holds the universal monopoly of religious tolerance has been disturbed. As Levi-Strauss has pointed out: "Thus Islam, which invented tolerance in the Near East, cannot forgive non–Muslims for not abjuring their faith and joining Islam, since it has the crushing superiority over all other faiths that it respects them."[1] The irony of this passage is, as one might suspect, very displeasing to those Westerners who have assumed the role of "public relations" agents for Islam. The claim to a monopoly of tolerance, of course, falls of its own weight, without considering the fact that even if Islam had found the means of guaranteeing the happiness of its Jews and Christians, the problem of the other non–Muslims would remain. According to the narrow interpretation still given by most Islamic jurists of the Koran and traditional texts, they have no right to the *dhimma*—the "protection" of Islam—and, if they are in Muslim power, can choose only between death and conversion to Islam, or perhaps conversion to Judaism or Christianity.

The response, even of uneducated Near–Easterners is to shift the conversation with the foreigner concerned with the current situation of minorities living in Arab lands—including Muslims like Kabyles and Kurds—into the domain of history. "How dare you accuse us of discrimination against our Christian compatriots? By what right do you speak of persecutions[2] by us, when you had the Inquisition?" This is what I heard, in angry tones, form Egyptian students, teachers and government officials after I began to publish reports in 1977 on anti–Copt assaults in Egypt. I had, however, been careful to show that these were isolated incidents, even if they had become more frequent, that should be attributed not to Muslims in general but to extremists who claimed to represent Islam.

Apparently, even this was too much. Even among educated men, acquainted with Western culture, themselves critical of their own society, very lukewarm toward religious practices, and proclaiming themselves modernists, the reflex of Islamic solidarity, to my great surprise, was stronger than the sense of simple justice owed to their Christian fellow citizens, if only to the extent of allowing a foreign journalist to report events that he had witnessed. As I persisted in writing about a subject that was tragically in the news from 1979 to 1981, my relations with several Muslim friends cooled, even with those who were on the "left," while countless government doors were closed to me, in the Ministries of Information, Culture, and Economy, and in the President's staff.

The Lebanese–Palestinian conflict sometimes took on a real, but unexpressed, religious coloration, but this was less in the streets of Beirut than in pan–Arab institutions and conferences entrusted with resolving the war. Despite the very strong sympathies of Lebanese Christians for the West, regimes as troubled by Soviet advances in their area as post–Nasser Egypt and Saudi Arabia could never bring themselves to offer massive and open aid to the Christian resistance. Even though the Palestinians frightened the other Arabs because of their links with communist Europe or their revolutionary or Marxist rhetoric, in the eyes of Riyadh, Cairo and other pro–Western Arab–Muslim capitals, they were first of all Muslims. If there was a decisive religious aspect to the war in Lebanon, this was it, and it helped only the Palestinians, since the "Christian" West did anything but support non–Muslim Lebanese.

The Moroccan writer, Tahar Ben Jelloun, a righteous and secular spirit, refused to speak out against the destruction of the Beirut section of Achrafieh by Syrian bombs in the summer of 1978—"For the love of these Christian Arabs who yesterday revived the Arab literature and were the first to illustrate the Arab nationalism, cry out in favor of their massacred descendants." Without a doubt, this refusal stemmed from his more or less conscious obsession of not offending the umma while taking a position, even on a strict humanitarian basis, in favor of the non-Muslims.

In the spring of 1981, who in the West demonstrated or circulated petitions for the children of Zahle dying under Syrian artillery attacks? Who called for help for that little Christian town in the Bekaa valley, under attack since 1975 by Arab forces not from Lebanon? One could fill a large book with all the appeals and motions inspired throughout the world with ample justification, in 1976 by the siege of Tell–Zaatar, a fortified Palestinian enclave within the largerChristian enclave.

But in 1981, I noted only a single important statement for Zahle when it was under attack: the Christian Democratic Party asked the Rome government to urge "the European Community to take concrete and humanitarian initiatives [which it of course failed to do] to assist the exhausted Lebanese people." The communique even pointed out that "the democratic governments of the European countries are witnessing the massacre of Lebanese Christians without taking any political or diplomatic steps to put an end to genocide of a people living in terror. Since these are Christians whom the current forces in Lebanon wish, for political reasons, to eliminate physically, these crimes have gone unremarked. If these crimes had been perpetrated against non-Christians, we would already have seen expressions of outrage, appeals, marches, and protests from those who claim to struggle for human rights."

With some individual exceptions, the Christian world has never been concerned with the fate of the Lebanese Christian community, which has struggled alone (except for unreliable and shifting support from Israel and Syria), fighting for each house, each tree, each rock. And why should the Catholics of Toulouse, Paris, or Brussels have been moved by the Maronites, when newspapers and radio stations constantly repeated that they were "fascists," "reactionaries," or at best "conservatives"? This was a remarkable enterprise of disinformation in which the professional Muslims had the lion's share, concealing the fact that the social program of the Falange (a movement with an unfortunate name, to be sure) was inspired by the Christian personalism of Emmanuel Mounier. It is undeniable that shaykh[3] Bashir Gemayel added "muscle" to the party founded by his father Pierre and gave it a populist flavor, but if he hadn't it is likely that Lebanon would no longer exist and that almost all the Christians would have been transported to Canada, as the United States wished in 1976.

Muslims are less particular on questions of religious solidarity. To take only two examples, the *umma* supported to the end the bloody dictator of Uganda, Idi Amin, who now lives peacefully in Saudi Arabia, and it was united around the no less bloody Jean–Bedel Bokassa of the Central African Republic, during the period when he called himself a Muslim. After he returned to Christianity, he was abandoned.

While the problems posed by the existence of minorities within Islamic societies are more or less well known in Lebanon and Iran, because of particularly violent events—apparently the only means of attracting the attention of the outside world—those problems in Egypt have traditionally been ignored. The very presence in the country of a native community of Christians, larger than all the other Christian communities of the Arab Near East and Asia Minor combined, is usually not mentioned in general works or atlases about the area published in the West; not to mention works on Egypt, published there or elsewhere, presenting the country as religiously homogeneous, or noting the Coptic phenomenom, which involves several million people, only as a residual curiosity.

Pierre Loti, in 1908, described the Copts he saw in the alleys of Old Cairo as "archaic Christians." A man as cultivated as André Gide, cruising on the Nile between Aswan and Wadi Halfa in January 1946, noted: "Villages the color of earth, sand, rock; villages that I suppose are Coptic."[4] There had never been any Copts in the region, where the only Christians had been the Nubians, who disappeared after the Arab conquest; the city of Aswan, the border between Nubia and Egypt proper, now has a Coptic colony, but from Said—the north. Before Gide, European travelers in the Nile Valley, as far back as the Middle Ages, with a few exceptions, showed little interest in their Egyptian co–religionists (it is true that Catholics considered the Copts to be schismatics), generally talking only of their shortcomings. Thévenot, in his *Narrative of a Journey to the Levant*, in 1664, complained that they were "very ignorant and coarse people." The German Dominican in Colbert's service, Vansleb, in his *New Narrative of a Journey to Egypt*, in 1672–1673, noted that "there is no longer anyone among them who can gain recognition from the Turks for his intelligence." The Venetian doctor Prosper Alpino, in *The Natural History of Egypt*, (1581–1584),[5] was alone in trying to find the reasons for this decadence: "If the Copts recognized the authority of the Roman pontiff, they would surpass our Christians in everything, for they defend our faith with so much energy that they are ready to withstand any insults for the name of Christ and, although they live under the power of infidels and are daily showered with insults, affronts, blows, and profound contempt, and are often despoiled of their goods, nevertheless, they in no way wish to replace their faith in Christ with belief in Mohammed. And yet, if they did so, they would be relieved from these troubles and would gain a calm and peaceful life. But they prefer to be Christians in the greatest servitude rather than to abandon their faith in order to rule."

Closer to our time, in his *Doctor Ibrahim*, (1937), the Swiss novelist John Knittel (1891–1970), who had lived in Egypt, has one of his Muslim characters say: "Copt, you're a weakling from birth." And the surrealist writer Georges Henein, whose father was a Copt, but who had been shaped by his Italian mother and his French education, wrote: "For the Copt, the meaning of death has nothing that is poignant. It is a form of vengeance, a habit of taking vengeance on everything. It is not true that the Copt is pursued by the Muslim. He is pursued only by the idea of scandal. He hides openly. An obsessive termite, he grows the bitter weeds of a resignation that finally becomes aggressive. The Coptic sigh, the bewildered look of the Copt, his need in all things to be crouched in his lair coated with old poisons are signs of an identity that wills itself to be irremediable." And referring to a friend who had died young: "He died at his post, in the skin of a consenting slave. The family, the Coptic family, where the canary gives up singing, closed in on him, enveloped him alive in the shroud of desolation."[6]

His detachment from his origins and his conversion to Islam because of his marriage (juridically valid even though it had no meaning for an agnostic) did not succeed in removing the Coptic stamp from Georges Henein in the eyes of the Muslims. His widow, Iqbal, granddaughter of the great Muslim poet Ahmad Shawqi (his statue is at the villa Borghese in Rome with those of Goethe and Byron), wanted to make a gift to the state of her husband's library, unique in Egypt, with thousands of old and modern French books. She went to see the Minister of Culture in 1978. Her only condition was that the room in the Ahmad Shawqi museum where the bequest was to be installed bear the inscription: "Library of Georges Henein given to the Shawqi museum by his wife Iqbal, granddaughter of Ahmad Shawqi." "No, madam, it is not possible to put the names Georges between your grandfather's name and yours." Scandalised by this sectarian approach to culture, Mme. Henein left. The Egyptian state will never inherit the books of George Henein, who should have been named Mohammed, Ali, or Mustafa. Anecdotal histories of literature will perhaps recall that Henein had chosen a Muslim name when he was "converted," Bayazid; but the employee who was supposed to register it had said: "It's too complicated. Keep Georges."

The Coptic academician Magdi Wahba spoke one day of the "sterile anguish" of his community, compared to the anguish of the Jews, fertile in the sense that it had led to the creation of Israel. This absence of illusions, this kind of pity that certain Copts feel for their own community, the lack of interest or deliberate ignorance, or else denigration and contempt, continue to be present. A subject people, the Copts have also been forgotten by history, without enjoying the happiness which is supposed to accompany that situation. Even today, when the western intelligentsia hunts throughout the world for dying cultures and assassinated civilizations to demand reparation in their name, no voice has been raised to denounce the "cultural genocide," the "removal from the historical stage" of the Coptic nation.

Christian survival in Egypt is an enigma. The mountains of Lebanon explain Maronite resistance, and Jurjura explains the survival of the Kabyles. The level vally of the Nile can conceal no resistance nor can it provide refuge. Unless it is a "miracle," the persistence of this population in remaining Coptic, while joining Islam does so much to simplify life in the Arab East, can only be analyzed in the light of the cult of loyalty to origins that appears elsewhere, among the French Canadians and the Poles. Like them, the Egyptian Copts owe their survival to themselves alone.

The only serious historical study of the Copts, based principally on Muslim sources, was written by Jacques Tagher.[7] Because of this work, its author was dismissed as King Faruq's librarian. He died shortly afterward in a mysterious accident. His book was and remains banned, and fundamentalists continue to pursue it thirty years after its publication.

For political reasons, Bonaparte in Egypt proclaimed himself a Muslim. The Nile valley was certainly worth a *shahada.*[8] "Aren't we the ones who destroyed the pope who said that we had to make war againts the Muslims? Aren't we the ones who destroyed the Knights of Malta, because those madmen believed that God wanted them to wage war against the Muslims?" he proclaimed to the Egyptian people, before donning a turban to go to the mosque to sit devoutly among the *ulama* listening to the recitation of the life of the Prophet. He wrote to a Cairo theologian, Shaykh el–Messiri: "I hope that it will not be long before I can establish a uniform system based on the principles of the Koran, which alone are true and are alone capable of making men happy."

A member of the Muslim Brotherhood speaking today could not be clearer than the future emperor seized by demagogic zeal. To be more convincing, he thought it worth noting his contempt for the Copts, going so far as telling his subordinates: "Never hesitate to give preference to Muslims over Christians;" and in the instructions he left for Kléber before he returned to France in August 1799: "Whatever you do to them, the Christians will always be for us." After making contrary promises to a Coptic official who had pleaded his community's cause, according to a reliable Muslim chronicler, Abd al-Rahman al-Jaborti, restored the requirement that Christians wear a black or blue turban and not smoke, drink, or eat in public during Ramadan, "in order not to disturb the fasting Muslim." Moreover, he gradually began to remove Copts from the technical and financial occupations that they had traditionally been assigned to by the Muslim rulers of Egypt. The celebrated *Description of Egypt*, an encyclopedic work published by the scholars and scientists of the expedition after their return to France, a work which the Arabs had until recently refused to publish in their language because of the space given to the "time of idols"—Pre–Islamic Egypt—will charm Muslim fundamentalists when they read that "greed and avarice, the only motives for all the actions [of the Copts], has removed them too far from love of science and the arts for them to feel the slightest desire to distinguish themselves in those fields."

Since Bonaparte's flirtation with Islam was purely a masquerade, these almost racist calumnies of Egyptian Christians finally had no effect on the minds of Egyptian Muslims, who never stopped seeing the French as incurable unbelievers occupying their country. The three years of French domination might, however, have had serious consequences for the Christians of Egypt, because of the obscure episode of the Coptic Legion, something that the Muslim Brotherhood has recently unearthed and reinterpreted in order to increase the gulf between the two Egyptian religious communities.

When the French arrived in Egypt in 1798, it seems that the director of finance Ya'qub, in contrast with his more delicate co–religionists, was the only Copt who had been able to wrest from the reigning Mamelukes the right to bear arms, which was then denied to non–Muslims. Put at the service of Desaix by the new French masters of the country, Ya'qub recruited and equipped, at his expense, a corps of auxiliaries made up of eight hundred Copts. Without explaining clearly what it was all about, from the most miserable Christian villages of Upper Egypt, with false promises of money, or simply kidnapping, he recruited a few hundred young Coptic fellahs, illiterate, unused to the profession of arms for more than ten centuries, and stunned to find themselves in the uproar of Cairo. According to the historian al-Jabarti: "Recruited in the south, their dark complexion, added to their natural filth and their awful caps (in black sheepskin), made them really ugly to see." On the other hand, there is no record of any participation of this Coptic Legion in battles in alliance with the French; in fact, it lasted for only a few months and its members disbanded even before the French capitulation.

The story has nevertheless persisted, and it is almost always presented from a perspective that is damaging to the Copts. The Copts would be well advised to remember—as the Muslim al-Jabarti, among other sources, reports—that the pitiful Coptic Legion was merely a belated imitation of Muslim contingents—Maghribis or Mamelukes—who had on several occasions fought against their brother Muslims under French command. They had suffered no condemnation, even though they did not have the extenuating circumstance of sharing religious belief with the invaders.

The British occupation, from 1882 to 1922, was as a whole scarcely more beneficial to the Copts, even though the frequency of English first names among lower class Copts might suggest a certain nostalgia. French first names are in any event more widespread.[10] In reality, entrenched in their orthodoxy, the Copts always resisted submitting to the English as well as the French, in whom they saw, not without reason, propagators of Protestantism and Catholicism respectively.

The establishment at the end of the last century of the Coptic Catholic and Coptic Evangelical churches, each of which had about 150,000 members in 1983, indicates that the fears of orthodox Copts were not groundless. Even since the 1973 Vatican meeting between Pope Paul VI and Shenuda III, in the course of which it was agreed to put an end to inter–Christian proselytism in Egypt, the distrust of orthodox Copts for Catholics has not completely disappeared: Catholics who marry orthodox Copts have to be re–baptized. Even though Shenuda III defined the position of his sect in relation to Catholicism with the formula: "Unity of faith, diversity of administration," ecumenical rapprochement has remained rather incomplete, even though the national Egyptian church can no longer be called monophysite—the doctrine that Christ was only divine not human, adopted by the Copts in the fifth century essentially to express their political opposition to Byzantine domination over Egypt. All current Coptic missals indicate that the Alexandrian pontiff and his flock recognize the dual nature, human and supernatural, of the Messiah.

In the Arab Near East, France was always intent on aiding the Christians; it created modern Lebanon, the first and only Arab state in history to establish real juridical equality between Muslims and non-Muslims, and it promoted a Greek Orthodox premier for Syria, Faris al-Khuri.[11] England, on the other hand—because of its "romanticism" according to Lawrence Durrell, from cold reason according to others—constantly expressed a clear preference for the Muslims, against the Maronites (in the Levant in the nineteenth century), the Copts (in Egypt at the turn of the century), and the Assyrians (in Mesopotamia between the wars). A character in *Mountolive* says: "Now Egypt is freed from the English hatred of the Copts. The English encouraged the Muslims to oppress us. They infected the Muslims with their contempt for the Copts." Although English indifference to the Copts had negative effects in the immediate, that very fact later turned in their favor during the 1919 Anti-British revolution, during which Christians played the principal political role, unusual in light of local customs and disproportionate in their numerical strength.

Present day Islamic fundamentalists want to erase this episode from the national history and they buy up and destroy any publication that describes the role played by Christians during this decisive period in the development of modern Egypt. In 1922, the last year of the British protectorate, seven Egyptians were condemned to death for nationalist activities. The names of all seven are unmistakably Coptic, and the fundamentalists will have great difficulty in obliterating them from history.

The slightest suspicion of collaboration with the occupiers would have prohibited the Christians from taking leading roles in the independence struggle. Minorities always have an interest in avoiding grounds for the slightest suspicion. The Muslim nationalist historian Mohammed Sabri wrote in his *Révolution Egyptienne*[12] that the Copts, in 1919–21, were "among the most ardent supporters of the nationalist idea, and the first victims to fall in the cause of independence." This did not prevent the Muslim Brotherhood from later casting doubt on the patriotic or non–collaborationist attitude of the Copts under both the French and the English. This was pure calumny, but as we all know since Beaumarchais, "the harm is done, it grows, it creeps, it walks," until it reaches "hatred and proscription."

Copts who have received Western higher education are more able than their equally educated Muslim counterparts to extract themselves from the swamp of sectarianism that oppresses the minds of Egyptians from childhood on. Although they did so much later than their co–religionists who emigrated from Syria and Lebanon to Egypt in the nineteenth century, the Copts gradually became integrated into the capitalist system, since they were not restrained by the Muslims' fundamental rejection of the banking system inspired by the Prophet's attacks against usury. For the same reason, the Copts have remained the only repository of the ancient Egyptian financial tradition, particularly in matters of accounting. They have been, and continue to be, pushed into the private sector because there they encounter less of the religious obstacles that prevent them from succeeding in public service.

Consequently, during periods of extension of state control, as under Nasser, Christians were generally more harmed (proportionally) than Muslims by measures of control, nationalization, and confiscation. However, although there were great Coptic fortunes on the eve of the 1952 revolution, the symbol of private economic success was the Muslim big businessman who established the powerful industrial banking group Misr in 1920, Talaat Harb, whom Nasser himself honored with a statue in the heart of modern Cairo.

Under Sadat, the return to market economics was, of course, favored by the Copts, since significant promotions within the administration were extremely rare for them. Nevertheless, the real millionaires remained members of the majority religion, like the public works and building contractors Osman Ahmad Osman and Hasan Allam. In any event, as the moralist and traveler Volney said to Bonaparte, "the Christian in the East has no interest in developing his talents, because the more he does the more he will be persecuted." The statement may be excessive, but it is not always an exaggeration to say that too visible a success or too public a fortune are more generally harmful to a Christian than to a Muslim in the Eastern Mediterranean.

The pejorative expression (explicable only by the fact that blue was for a while a color imposed on Christians in the Islamic world) "blue bone," identifying a Copt, seems to have been used especially in Alexandria between 1920 and 1950, when it was noted by the Franco-Egyptian novelist Jean Dideral.[13] Hence, it is not suprising that the Italian poet Giuseppe Ungaretti, born in Alexandria in 1888, wrote in 1931:[14] "Let us talk a little about the Copts, those small-eyed, anemic, pushy men. Miserly, sober, and deceitful, they love fish, *fasikh*,[15] caught at the mouth of the Nile and left to 'ripen' in the mud. The odors of this decay infest the air for miles around. Perhaps the Pharaohs appreciated it." And Ungaretti concludes scornfully: "From the first great adventure of the West, only these eaters of garbage have survived." In *Monsieur Zéro*,[16] Paul Morand describes Macaire, the Coptic interpreter, as "vindictive like his fellows," and naturally, "a government informer."

This unanimity of hostility and malevolence toward a people—for the sake of completeness, we should mention the very recent "literature" of the Egyptian fundamentalists, describing Coptic "fortress churches" overflowing with weapons "intended to kill Muslims," "anti-Islamic Israeli-Coptic collusion," and Christian doctors who "refuse to give anesthesia before operations or tourniquets for bleeding" to Muslim patients—is almost without equal in our day, now that the Israeli nation has reversed the persecution of which the Jews were victims for two thousand years, and almost everywhere oppressed minorities bring forth help and sympathy. The Copts cannot even claim the palm of martyrdom. The conscience of the world is stirred by an exodus, a massacre, a genocide. It does not notice a silent ethnic group, slandered in small doses and denied for centuries. Even the Algerians, who loudly profess "tolerance" for the last European Christians in their country, have harassed the Copts: in January 1981 they closed the Church used by the community of Egyptian Christian aid workers in Algiers. The only reaction in Paris was a few lines in two or three newspapers, much less than if the victims had been Jews or Muslims.

Even death does not call this double standard that always operates against the Copts into question. In the summer of 1981, two terrorist attacks occurred almost simultaneously, with the same number of victims, one in the square in front of a Cairo church where a Coptic popular wedding was taking place, the other in a Vienna synagogue where a holiday was being celebrated. The Vienna incident properly provoked prominent denunciation in the world press, while the blood of the Copts merited only brief mention in the back pages. Most of the world is now sensitive to the slightest sign of anti-Semitism. On the other hand, in Egypt, since 1972, churches have regularly been burned, Christians have been robbed, insulted, and killed, and to punish them for having protested against their ill treatment at the hands of the Muslim activists, Sadat threw priests, bishops, and even the patriarch Shenuda III in prison. The file on the Copts is so filled with evidence that is damning for their detractors that it has become almost suspect. Respected voices could at least have attempted to draw attention to it out of a sense of honor; only the Orthodox writer of Russian origin, Gabriel Metzneff, expressed indignation that no Christian head of state had protested against the deposing of the patriarch of Alexandria, "while one can easily imagine the emotion that would stir us if we were to learn that the President of the Italian Republic had deposed the Pope."[17] The great orientalist Louis Massignon once told Father Pierre du Bourguet, a Jesuit specialist on the Copts: "The Copts are victims. It is through them that Egypt will be saved." One has the impression that Christians in the West, to the extent that they are aware of Coptic suffering, see it as an inevitability, corresponding too closely to their idea of redemptive sacrifice for them to intervene.

Finally, it seems that only Mohammed himself wished the Copts well. The Prophet, one of whose concubines was Mariya the Copt, the only woman of his harem who produced a viable son, was supposed to have said of the child, who died at three: "If he had lived, I would not have allowed a single Copt to pay the poll tax." There are a whole series of Mohammed's sayings, one more laudatory and friendly than the other, on the Egyptian Christians whom Mohammed probably knew only through a single woman. "Be obliging to the Copts, you will find them of great help in combating your enemies." "First, you are going to conquer the Copts, then they will help you to realize God's designs." "The Copts are our relatives, they will help you in your religion."

Arab–Muslim chroniclers and "traditionists"[18] even report with complete seriousness that in answer to his disciples who expressed surprise that non–Muslims could help them, Mohammed said: "The Copts will attend to the things of this world, thus allowing you to devote yourselves to prayer." It is hard not to recall this saying when one sees the Islamic states of the Arabian peninsula functioning thanks to cohorts of Lebanese, Palestinians, and Egyptians among whom are many Christians.

A simple glance in Muslim annals reveals that, through the centuries, neither the spirit nor the letter of the recommendations about the Copts attributed to Mohammed has been respected. More than thirteen centuries of *dhimma*—the status that should be called "submission" rather than "protection," since the latter was often absent, while the former was seldom challenged—have shaped the psychology of the Christians of Egypt; it is a mixture of prudence, reserve and fear, especially fear; a mixture of treachery and cowardice according to those who have not lived the Coptic experience from within. This experience is hardly comparable to the life of the Christians of the Levant, who have always been able to use the mountainous terrain of their country more or less to escape from dhimma and to maintain some links with the rest of Christendom. In April 1982, in Bayt–Miri, a village overlooking Beirut which was then under Syrian and Palestinian control, Beshir Gemayel told me, as he had earlier, in June 1976, in Ashrafiya, under the "Islamic progressive" bombs: "Attacked as Christians, we reacted as Lebanese. The existence of a Lebanon in which Christians are not subject to *dhimma* is for us a question of life or death." And after a pause, he added: "If one day we have to choose between Brezhnev and Khomeini, we will choose Brezhnev without hesitation."

Their situation of total exposure to the will or the whims of masters who bear a culture, a language, an ideology, a religion, and customs that were from the outset almost totally foreign to the Pharaonic, Greco–Roman, and Christian heritage of Egypt, explains why the Copts, ethnically not Arab, are now the most Arabized Christians in the Near East, the most eastern, the most integrated into the Muslim world. It also explains why Coptic art, that was so promising, to judge by what has survived in the great museums of the world or in Egypt itself, died out; why the Coptic language is now only a liturgical or archaic idiom; why the incredible theological richness of Egyptian Christianity (Clement, Origen, Athanasius, Anthony, Paul, Pacoma, Shenuda, and other Church fathers and saints) dried up after the intrusion of Islam.

But regrets are pointless. One civilization expels another, "It is the common currency of History," as the fatalist Paul Morand noted. The Arab–Islamic colonization also brought a great deal to Egypt. History is made up of the ebb and flow of cultures, some of them inexorably having to disappear for the benefit of others, which are not necessarily greater. On the other hand, what ought to be regretted and denounced is the manipulation of history. Open any Egyptian or Arab school book, and you will see a few cursory lines, if there are any at all, which skate over the five or six centuries of Christian Egypt, wedged between the "evil" glory of the idolatrous Pharaohs and the "good" glory of the devout caliphs. The Arabization and Islamization of the Nile valley is presented as a painless operation. Every time I come across the "pious humbug" that the Muslims were greeted by the Copts as liberators, I am reminded of Voltaire's complacent sentence: "The Gauls were happy to be conquered by the Romans." On the contrary, the conquest in depth of Egypt was carried out with the fire and sword of rebellion, coercion, and financial extractions. The Copts, it is true, are now culturally and mentally

Arabs and, in the realm of customs and behavior, there is no great detectable difference between them and their Muslim compatriots. Indeed, most of the latter are descendants of Copts who converted to Islam. There is, however, a quality of sadness characteristic of the Christians of the Nile, an atavistic melancholy that overlays all their joys and even makes their wedding ceremonies and Christmas masses almost funeral ceremonies. The minister Boutros–Ghali, after accompanying Sadat to a prayer ceremony at al–Aqsa mosque in Jerusalem in November 1977 (he was the only Copt present except for the journalist Musa Sabri), told me: "Palestinian Islam is sad, one can see that it is an Islam under domination." He did not realize, perhaps, that he had felt in Palestine what every foreign Christian could experience in a Coptic ceremony in Egypt. The Egyptian-Lebanese Jesuit father Henri Habib Ayrout, founder of free schools that have largely helped to bring upper Egypt out of obscurantism in the twentieth century, recognized Christian fellahs by their look, despite their resemblance to Muslim fellahs. In the eye of the Copt, there are fourteen centuries of uncertainty and anxiety. "Only those who are used to draining the chalice to the dregs can have eyes like that. Jesus on the cross certainly had those eyes." This observation by Franz Werfel about the Armenians of Turkey, in *The Forty Days of Mussa–Dagh*, is more or less valid for all the Christians of the East, and above all for the Copts.

The most serious reproach, in the end the only important one, that can be addressed, since the Islamic conquest of the country, if not to all the leaders at least to all Egyptian regimes, is that they were never able or willing to provide permanent physical and psychological security for their non–Muslim citizens. An exception must however be made, to a large extent, for the dynasty of Mohammed Ali (1804–1953) and for the secular nationalist party Wafd from 1922–1952.

The harassment, thefts, brutality, and even assassinations that the Jews of Egypt and almost all the other Islamic states had to endure after the creation of Israel in 1948 are strikingly similar to medieval narratives written by the Muslims themselves relating the murders and brutality perpetrated on the Copts by soldiers or the general populace when Islam seemed to be threatened from outside by a foreign Christian force, like the crusades. Sometimes, the simple greed of a sultan, an emir, a group of mercenaries, or a faction of the people, or else the fanaticism and ignorance of an unusually eloquent preacher in the mosque, was enough to provoke a riot or a *ukase* against native Christians, and sometimes also against the Jews. We should note in this connection that, in Egypt, there seems never to have been any real effort of mutual aid between Jews and Christians, perhaps because the Copts are not always free of anti–Judaism. In October 1977, at the laying of the cornerstone for Saint Mark Hospital, on the site of the Orthodox Copt patriarchate in Cairo, Shenuda III recited, like a litany in front of Sadat, the verses from the Koran and the Sunna hostile to the Jews, which was all the more absurd because the entire audience could have drawn anti–Christian quotations from the same texts.

From the "Magnanimous" Caliph Omar—who at first suggested that "Egypt should be left as it is," and then, contrary to the customs of the time, demanded from living Christians the special tax of the *dhimmi* owed by the dead, on the pretext that the Copts "were conquered by force of arms and were thus in the category of slaves"—to Sadat, who at first flattered his non–Muslim compatriots, and then, without warning, loudly and repeatedly proclaimed one day on radio and television: "I am the Muslim president of a Muslim country," as though they did not exist, and in another speech, insulted and deposed their patriarch as a Merovingian king would have deposed a bishop. In contrast, one could cite a hundred past and present examples of benevolence and help from Muslims, sovereigns, ministers, or simple citizens, for the Copts. When there were fundamentalist attacks against the Copts under Sadat, I gathered evidence from several people that proved that Muslims had saved Christians and prevented their churches and homes from being burned. Nevertheless, that changes nothing in the basic situation.

The Fatimid Caliph al-Aziz (976–996), no doubt the most benevolent of the dynasty, even wanted to bring about equality between Christians and Muslims in his empire. He personally had churches built, and went so far as to send troops to disperse Islamic extremists who wanted to prevent the restoration of the sanctuary of Saint Mercurios in Cairo. Moreover, the caliph refused to punish Muslims who converted to Christianity or former Christians who returned to their original religion.

The Copts breathed. They thought that their ordeal was over. Aziz died. He was succeeded by his son, al-Hakim, age eleven. Titled the "Ruler by Order of Allah," he inaugurated his coming of age by confirming the dhimmi officials appointed by his father, following the advice of his sister, who was known for her sympathy for the Copts and may herself have been a secret Christian. The young caliph engaged a Copt as secretary. And then, one fine day, he had him assassinated. The wheel had turned. A Christian dignitary was summoned immediately to profess faith in Islam under penalty of death. Most Coptic officials were dismissed. Discriminatory signs on clothing were again imposed on Christians, who no longer had the right to employ Muslims. An edict ordered the destruction and pillage of all the churches of the Fatimid kingdom, including the Holy Sepulcher in Jerusalem. Thirty thousand Christian buildings are reported to have been destroyed or damaged. The orthodox monasteries of Wadi Natrun, forgotten in the desert, were almost alone to escape from the Egyptian disaster. Sadat imprisoned the patriarch Shenuda III in one of them in 1981, under the army's surveillance.

Non–Muslim celebrations were forbidden, foundations for the benefit of churches or convents were nationalized before the term was invented, and the little crosses that Copts traditionally tatooed on their right wrists so that they would be buried in the right place if they died away from home had to be removed, while large wooden crosses weighing five pounds, by regulation, were hung on the necks of all Christians. They even lost the right to use the services of a donkey man or ferry crosser. The crowd was incited to violate Coptic cemeteries, and the bones dug up were used to heat the water in Cairo *hammams*. The list is not exhaustive.

The very reliable Muslim historian al-Maqrizi relates that al-Hakim finally ordered all his Christian subjects to go into exile in the territory of the Byzantine Empire. In his annals, the Christian chronicler Yahya al-Antaqi sketches a scene that he located in Cairo in 1012 in front of the Caliph's palace. We see a long procession of Coptic notables—scribes, apothecaries, doctors, fired officials, priests, and prelates—"walking bare–headed, barefoot, asking forgiveness, and weeping, kissing the earth until they had arrived at the palace. They presented a petition to a courtier begging for al-Hakim's clemency, and he finally delivered safe–conduct letters to them." But the next day, new cruelties were dreamed up against the Christians, many of whom preferred to deny their faith to obtain a little bit of tranquility.

The ups and downs of Coptic history would produce an endless narrative. The same highs and lows recurred under Saladin, who so charmed the Franks that they gave his name to their children, but who at home made the Copts suffer dearly, prefiguring Sadat's ambivalence. The Mamelukes, in 1320, as though by a pre-arranged signal, fell on the "miscreants" throughout the country, pillaging and destroying churches "down to their foundations," getting drunk on mass wine, ravaging nuns and killing resisters. Since Christians at the time had to wear white turbans, Sultan al-Nasir Mohammed ibn Qalawun proclaimed that any Muslim who met a man wearing such a turban in the streets of Cairo could kill him and seize his goods.

In 1785, the Ottomans, suddenly prohibited the Copts from having horses or slaves (the slave trade was still free in Egypt), from dressing like Muslims and from having the names of the prophets Abraham (Ibrahim), Moses (Musa) and Jesus (Isa).

Blowing hot and cold, the entire history of the Copts from the seventh century to the present has followed that pattern. It is impossible to say that there has been a single generation in fourteen centuries that has lived with its mind at ease. The Copts have always been on the alert, since the favor or the simple calm of a just reign was always spoiled by anxiety over the inevitable reversal of direction. They have always known, to paraphrase Cesare Pavese, that "the most secretly and horribly feared thing" would happen to them one day. This Coptic anxiety goes hand in hand with resignation in the face of past degradation and present semi–citizenship. They represent an extreme case of a population whose masters have almost methodically degraded them and now look down on them from the heights of their good conscience; a "perfectly typical case of cultural alienation," to adopt the jargon of sociologists; a case that interests no one, for in the Arab East one must hold closely to the "masses," that is, the Muslims, even when they join the Muslim Brotherhood. As for Muslim intellectuals, including those who have drifted toward religious indifference or atheism, they refuse, with few exceptions, to look reality in the face or even to open the Muslim archives; they are too afraid that they would find there what they know vaguely but do not want to admit: the centuries long injustice imposed on the Copts by Egyptian Islam.

If a Copt forgets that he is a Copt, a whole network of habits, obligations, and automatisms is ready to remind him of that fact. In the higher political and intellectual spheres, it takes place gently. The same thing is not true in Coptic villages or suburbs, where every contact by a Christian with a representative of authority (perceived as "Islam") must be a reminder for the *dhimmi* of the fact that he is only tolerated. Naturally, it all takes place almost imperceptibly, and is invisible for the uninitiated, who might be outraged that the Coptic fellahs of Upper Egypt, speaking among themselves, sometimes call Muslims *kha'inun* —"traitors—in reference to their long past abandonment of Christianity. Of course, Muslim fellahs return the favor by saying that the Copts are "impious." But if the past remains so close, if people live in Egypt today as we would live in France with constant reference to the Wars of Religion of the sixteenth century; if, listening to young Copts, one would think the Islamic conquest took place yesterday, if the wounds have never been able to completely heal, this is because a whole system is present, refined in the course of centuries and thoroughly integrated with social mechanisms. The system reminds the Copt, daily, according to the historical period, of the precariousness or simply the limits of his rights.

Even anti-Christian violence has taken place for centuries according to a ritual whose unchanging character has ended by attenuating its hatefulness. In discovering an Arab manuscript of the fourteenth century relating "an anti–Christian riot in Qus"[19] (Upper Egypt), I had the impression of reading about life under Sadat. The Copts were punished for their "insolence" and their "plotting," following Islamic terminology that has remained unchanged through the centuries, like the resignation that determines that with every excess (insult, profanation, arson, assassination), the family, the street, the village, the Coptic community accept the blow with a slight ripple, just as a herd of antelopes will scatter for a moment then reform and move on when a lion has seized one of them for its prey. A few hours after the fatal explosion of a bomb in front of a Cairo church in the summer of 1981, the crowd of Christians was just as large and unconcerned. I did hear this observation from a young Coptic manager in a steel plant: "Don't see this as lack of concern or resignation, but only immense patience, an enormous inner strength based on prayer. This is how we have survived for centuries. This is what has delivered us from inner fear." Prayer, a virtue that has been forgotten in the West.

More prosaic and less educated, the manager's younger brother summed up the secret of Coptic endurance in another way: "Heads that are lowered are not cut off." And he explained further all the precautions that Christian tenants in a mixed building have to take to avoid dramatic explosions over the most banal disputes between neighbors.

This unhealthy climate will begin to change when the Egyptian government has stopped equivocating with the fundamentalists, when it no longer supports a sectarian system that is not openly acknowledged, when it has firmly said to those who are naive or hypocritical enough to believe that Mohammed bequeathed a recipe for society and government that is valid for all times and places: "We are a country in which faith in God is respected and encouraged, but it is a personal matter. Since all believers are equal in the eyes of God, discrimination purportedly based on religion is abolished." One might then see a

Coptic man marry a Muslim woman, testify for her in court, inherit from her, choose by agreement with her the religion of their children. An Egyptian would no longer have to reveal his religion to his examiner, his banker, or his employer, and the indication of religion that every Copt carries in his wallet or her handbag would disappear from identity papers. That would be the end of the Coptic problem. If there then arose a Muslim problem, this would be because Islam is a system definitively hostile to justice and happiness, something I certainly do not believe to be the case.

NOTES

1. Levi-Strauss, *Tristes Tropiques* (Paris, 1955).
2. I certainly never used so forceful and polemic a term as "persecution," which is, moreover, inaccurate to describe the current situation of Eastern Christians, particularly in Egypt. For them, things are more subtle and concealed.
3. The honorific Muslim title shaykh was given to certain Christian families of Lebanon in the Ottoman period.
4. *André Gide Journal*, 1942–1949 (Paris, 1950).
5. Prosper Alpino, *The Natural History of Egypt* (Cairo, 1980).
6. Extract from the unpublished diary of Henein, dated August 20, 1958 in Cairo, provided by his widow Iqbal.
7. *Coptes et musulmans* (Cairo, 1952), in French and Arabic with no publisher's name.
8. Islamic profession of faith: "There is no god but Allah, and Mohammed is the messenger of Allah."
9. *Merveilles biographiques et historiques*, French edition (Cairo, 1888).
10. A Syrian script writer of Egyptian films told me that whenever he gave one of his characters a Christian first name, even if it was typically Egyptian, the censors suppressed it. On the rare occasions when a Copt appears in Egyptian films, he is almost always an unsympathetic character. Even in everyday life, a Coptic first name is often a handicap; the influential Cairo journalists Hamdi Fu'ad and Musa Sabri could not have succeeded as they have if they had kept their original names Osiris and Shenuda beautiful as they are in the Egyptian context.

11. At the time, the Grand Mufti of the Syrian Republic had no hesitation in asserting from his pulpit that "a Chinese Muslim was closer to Syrian believers than Faris al-Khuri."
12. Mohammed Sabri, *Révolution Egyptienne* (Paris, 1921.)
13. Jean Dideral, *Egypte mes yeux mon Soleil* (Paris, 1968).
14. Giuseppe Ungaretti, *A partir du désert. Journal de voyage* (Paris, 1965).
15. This fish is in fact the buri *(mogil cephalus)*, a kind of mullet that lives in the Mediterranean and the salt lakes at the mouth of the Nile; this has from time immemorial been fermented and salted to prepare *fasikh*, which all Egyptians, without religious distinctions, eat with raw onions and lemon during the *Shamm al-Nasim*, the popular Egyptian festival celebrated on the Monday following the Greek Coptic Easter.
16. Paul Morand, *Monsieur Zéro* (Paris, 1936.)
17. *Le Monde*, November 7, 1981.
18. Specialists in the Sunna, the tradition of Mohammed.
19. *Annales islamologiques*, Institut français d'archéologie orientale (Cairo, 1980).

CHAPTER SIX

The Ra'is and the Patriarch

Timorous, confined, neurotic, perhaps having finally developed an unhealthy taste for their conditions, the Copts nevertheless found a way of clearly expressing their demands twice in the course of this century.

The first occasion was at the Coptic congress in Asyut, held in 1911 without authorization by the patriarch and influential Christian notables. The principal demands made on the Egyptian government, then under British control, were: recognition of Sunday as a holiday; an equitable distribution of administrative positions; representation of all elements of the population in elected assemblies; use of the provincial tax for the benefit of all Egyptians without distinction.

This meeting, which made a great stir at the time, was followed by a Muslim counter–congress in Heliopolis, a suburb of Cairo, organized by the English resident official Eldon Gorst, who accused the Copts of wanting "to split the Egyptian nation in two," as though it were not already split, and of supporting "the heresy of a state with two religions," as though it were not already a heresy to attribute a religion to the state.

Closer to our time, in 1978, was the long memorandum presented to Sadat by Mirrit Boutros–Ghali. Former senator and former minister, cousin of the Minister of State for Foreign Affairs Boutros Boutros–Ghali, Mirrit Boutros–Ghali acted on his own initiative. But, sensitive to the demands of his community, from the patriarch to the little people, he was able, in this document that was never distributed, to encompass all Coptic demands, of which some concrete examples follow.

1. Better justice for the Copts: Nasser's 1955 abolition of sectarian tribunals was good in principle, but its effect, since then, was that Christians have been judged by Muslims. This has sometimes brought about judgments that are not only unjust but insulting for the minority: "Christianity is the religion of unbelief" (a finding justifying a Christian mother's loss of custody of her children, after her husband had converted to Islam and repudiated her); "Islam is the best religion" (to take children away from a Christian father whose wife had converted to Islam); "You no longer exist, you are legally dead" (to a young Muslim woman who had married a Christian outside the country, had adopted his religion, and had returned with him to Egypt); "You may be polygamous" (to a Christian whose first wife had sued him for bigamy). The most aberrant cases, the most contrary both to particular Christian status, which remains in place, and to elementary justice, are legion.

2. Suppression of the ten conditions imposed by the administration since 1934 (codification of an old Ottoman rule from a time when the king of Egypt, candidate for the Caliphate, was already making concessions to the fundamentalists) for permission to build or repair a Church or a simple Christian prayer room, while the construction of mosques is not only unrestricted but a basis for tax relief. The procedure for churches is a veritable psychological torture for the Christian communities, since it can last for ten years without success. Since every building of the Christian faith must be built "at a respectful distance" from a mosque, it often happens that between the presentation of a request and the response, an Islamic building, by chance or through the sinister diligence of some fundamentalist

group, is built near the land chosen by the Copts. Everything has to begin again from the beginning, with no guarantee that the same misadventure will not recur. This law has been the origin of a large number of sometimes bloody incidents between communities; it is the most obvious symbol of the humiliating condition of the Christians in Egypt. This was recognized in 1972 by a joint commission of inquiry after the destruction by Muslims of the chapel of Khanka, near Cairo, a chapel that the Copts had established in a private house without official permission, because they were tired of waiting for an authorization that never came. Sadat nevertheless did not abrogate the law, simply promising Shenuda III that he would authorize him to build fifty churches rather than the thirty-five he had requested. In 1983, the Khanka chapel had not yet been rebuilt and, here and there in the country, "clandestine" churches are built in the hope of eventual authorization.

3. An end to Islamic proselytism, the only such activity allowed, while anything that bears the slightest resemblance to Christian propaganda is immediately and severely repressed. There are not many Coptic conversions to Islam—probably a few hundred each year—but they have for centuries produced a kind of slow hemorrhage that the Christian community has been prevented from stopping. Radio Cairo broadcasts thirty hours a day of Islamic programs on its different stations, and forty-five minutes a week of Christian programs.

4. Restitution of the two hundred Coptic foundations (waqfs) confiscated in 1968 by the Ministry of Religious (Islamic) Endowments, whose beneficiaries no longer receive a penny (monasteries, churches, and especially Christian orphans, whose legal adoption is forbidden by Muslim law).

5. Recognition by the state of Coptic institutes, who will receive subsidies; abolition of religious discrimination in higher education, particularly in medicine. The Islamic university al-Azhar, financed by all taxpayers, is not open to Copts, even in its secular departments; among the dozen secular universities, none has a chair of Coptic language, considered to be "foreign." The number of Christians in the professional army, which was never very high, has further decreased in recent years as fundamentalists have denied Christians the right to bear arms.

6. In practice, no high administrative position is given to a Copt, the 360 nationalized companies being the most "favored," with ten directors' positions reserved for Christians in the late seventies; there are still two Coptic ministers in the government, but neither of them has any real domestic political weight; there was for a time under Sadat a Christian general in the army who had genuine command responsibilities, Fuad Aziz Ghali; he was later appointed governor of a province—a "first." But the province chosen was the least attractive, the poorest, and the most disagreeable in the country, southern Sinai.

I have had twenty conversations with the Coptic minister Boutros Boutros–Ghali. The only question I always avoided discussing seriously with him was that of his co–religionists, because I felt that he was trying to shake it off like a nightmare, even though, unlike many Egyptian Christians, he was thoroughly aware of the legitimacy of present–day demands for human rights, while simultaneously despairing of seeing those rights accorded to his fellow Copts in the near future. The career of the man who, with Sadat, was the Egyptian architect of peace with Israel provides a perfect symbol of the difficulty of being a Copt. In 1975, it was said of this international jurist, more valued in Geneva and New York than in his own country; "If he were not a Christian he would be ambassador to Paris or a minister in Cairo. What a shame that Egypt does not use such talent." Skeptical but patriotic, sociable without being too worldly, a hard worker without ostentation, this fifty year old man with the appearance of a student, heir of a long line of state officials, married to a distinguished Jewish woman from Alexandria, seemed a few years ago, despite his gifts, his intelligence, his cultivation, and his knowledge of world affairs and several languages, to be doomed to be nothing but a brilliant failure. Then came Sadat's journey to Jerusalem in November 1977, preceded by turmoil in Cairo in the course of which two Muslim ministers resigned from the Foreign Ministry in the space of a few hours. Very disappointed, the Ra'is, like several of his predecessor Caliphs or Sultans in other agitated periods, called on a Christian, in this case Boutros–Ghali. A few weeks earlier, he had held an obscure post in the Egyptian administrative hierarchy, supposedly charged with preparing "international conferences," but in fact created as a position for one of the two "token Copts" traditionally in the Egyptian cabinet.[1] "I accepted immediately because I have always been convinced that a negotiated solution was possible in the Near East," he said to me in the moments following his startling appointment as head of Egyptian foreign affairs.

No one in Cairo at the time thought that Sadat, preoccupied with appeasing the Muslim Brotherhood, would keep a Christian in such a visible position for very long. The minister of state was in fact appointed only as a provisional Minister of Foreign Affairs, and when Sadat and Begin met in Ismailia in December 1977, the Ra'is produced without warning a "head of Egyptian diplomacy," a slightly ridiculous functionary whose only virtue was to belong to the state religion, and whose name will certainly be forgotten by history. During the rough negotiations at Camp David in 1978, Sadat had to resign himself to the withdrawal of this timid minister. Butros-Ghali returned to the forefront. He was the only one on whom Sadat could rely to explain a question clearly, to prepare a complete dossier on time, and to untangle a complex problem of international law.

In order to "reward" Boutros-Ghali for his good and loyal services, after Camp David, the Ra'is appointed two successive nominal heads of the Foreign Affairs Ministry—Muslims, of course—above the unfortunate Coptic minister of state, who continued to carry on the real work: Mustafa Khalil, an icy technocrat who knew almost nothing about international relations; and then an apoplectic policeman-general, Kamal Hassan Ali, reappointed by Mubarak. All these snubs have had little effect on Boutros-Ghali, as though he had always foreseen them. But history will no doubt remember that, throughout the peace process launched by Sadat, a statesman saved others from disaster.

How is it possible to believe that Anwar al-Sadat—promoter of a dialogue among Muslims, Jews, and Christians in international affairs, an idea that he wanted to make concrete by launching a worldwide subscription for the construction in the Sinai of a center for prayer and meetings for the three religions, near which he even wanted to be buried—was able to tolerate an increase in religious discrimination in his own country? The answer is brief: like most of his fellow Muslims, the Ra'is did not see the "Christian compatriots," a little like those Frenchmen who express discreet prejudices against their Jewish compatriots while admiring the state of Israel. Sadat did not project onto his Western partners the prejudices hardened by centuries that the Muslim subconscious carries toward the Copts. Since the time of the Pharaohs, the Copts have borne a reputation as magicians and sorcerers which simultaneously attracts and repels every Egyptian who has not been imbued with rational influences. Although a Copt would never consult an imam (everyone would interpret this as a conversion to Islam), it is frequent and accepted that a Muslim with family, romantic, or legal problems will go to see the *abuna*—the Coptic priest—to learn some magical solution to his problem. But at the same time, the Muslims have an obscure sense that these pagan practices are proscribed by their religion, which leads to an ambiguous feeling toward the Copts.

Of course, such a contradictory situation has provoked among the Christians of Egypt simultaneous inferiority and superiority complexes. The Christian presence in the East, an indestructible vestigial community having survived against all odds in the Islamic ocean, is a living, permanent, and palpable reproach to the Muslims, who are deeply convinced of the obvious superiority of their faith over every other belief. While the Eastern Christians sometimes compare themselves to stars in the dark blue sky of Islam, Muslims cannot understand how these "islands of ignorance" have been able to resist the attraction of the "true religion" for fourteen centuries. Eastern Christendom is for them an "anomaly."

In May 1980, Sadat revealed that he had been in conflict with the patriarch Shenuda since September 1972, one year after his election as head of the Egypt Church. However, even after the collective fast of five days which he ordered his flock to carry on in September 1977 to protest against the government plan to restore capital punishment against temporary Christian converts to Islam (they generally convert to Islam for long enough to repudiate their wives, since divorce is forbidden to Christians in Egypt), the Ra'is continued to maintain relations with the Coptic hierarchy. In October 1977, having attended a wedding in a Coptic church a month before (an apparently unprecedented event), Sadat had asked the Patriarch to join him in prayer in the Patriarch's office. This unprecedented gesture had created an extraordinary stir among a population constantly attentive to religious signs, since Islamic custom required that a place sanctified by Muslim prayer could never again be used for the services of another faith.

While simple Copts were wondering whether the Muslim Brotherhood would one day demand that the Pope of Alexandria's office be turned into a mosque, more informed Christians predicted: "Sooner or later we will pay for our boldness," alluding to the protest fast. To be sure, this demonstration had been a bitter pill for the Ra'is because its spectacular character had called the attention of international public opinion to the Coptic question; it also informed many people throughout the world of the existence of several million non-Muslims in Egypt. Nevertheless, Sadat had rather easily agreed to forget the episode because his modernizing sensibility had to agree with his Christian compatriots in rejecting the proposed law of *ridda*—death for apostasy.

In 1978 and 1979, relations between Sadat and the Coptic church declined, with the church criticizing the Ra'is for doing nothing to stop the activities of the fundamentalists (notably, the assassination of a priest and his family, two bomb attacks during Orthodox Christmas celebrations in churches of Alexandria and the arson of the centuries-old shrine of the Virgin of al-Damshiriyya in Old Cairo), while the President saw Coptic demonstrations as the most likely means to stir up further problems with the fundamentalists. The most mortifying challenge to the government was the refusal of the Coptic church to celebrate Easter in 1980, as a protest against uncontrolled anti-Christian attacks, while the Patriarch refused to attend any ceremonies with the Ra'is and his ministers. Street demonstrations and advertisements in the U.S. press stigmatizing "the excesses of Islamic fanatics against the Copts" that the Egyptian president encountered on his visit to the United States in the spring of 1980 provoked him to cold anger, because they were exposing to his "American friends" the hidden disease of Egypt, the religious wound.

The Coptic community of North America, established in Nasser's time and containing several tens of thousands of members, having quickly learned the protest methods of their adopted country, were no doubt chiefly responsible for the tracts and marches, comparable to the anti–French demonstrations organized by American Jews in February 1970 during Pompidou's visit, to protest against France's pro–Arab policies. DeGaulle's successor did not take revenge for this affront on the chief rabbi of France. Sadat, appalled, was convinced that Shenuda III was behind the Coptic demonstrators in Washington who had seriously impaired his image as "father of a united Egypt." When he returned to Cairo in May 1980, he let it be known publicly that he had thought of deposing the Pope of Alexandria. From then on, Shenuda was blocked out of the media in Cairo and considered by Sadat's unconditional supporters as responsible for all the ills of the nation, starting with the more and more frequent attacks by Muslim fundamentalists against Christians. To exculpate himself, Shenuda circulated the cable he had addressed to his followers across the Atlantic during the visit of the Ra'is:

My beloved children abroad,

We love our church, we love our country, Egypt, to which all of us are loyal, and we all wish that its image be glowing everywhere.

The Copts are right to demand respect for their rights, but this should be done with wisdom and spirituality. We cannot accept any stain on the reputation of our country.

I ask you to receive the head of our beloved country, Anwar al–Sadat, with love and respect as we are taught by the Gospels and our conscience. If you have something to say to him, say it calmly and lovingly. Rest assured that he is doing much for the Copts, for the country, and for peace.

I have sent you my friends, Bishop Samuel and Bishop Jacob to talk with you and to calm the crisis.

May you prosper.

Shenuda III

The tension reached its paroxysm, and blood flowed between the Muslims and the Copts during the second half of June 1981, at Zawiyya al-Hamra, i.e. "Redchapel," as it had not for two centuries. This was one of the most miserable of Cairo's suburbs: blocks of subsidized housing, "spontaneous" houses made of half-baked bricks, poor shops, a few food and textile factories, unpaved streets, full of debris, crowded, and with a railroad track running through it. It was a suburb of Cairo almost clandestinely attached to Shubra, a lower class neighborhood that had once benefited from a kind of urbanization. In Zawiyya al-Hamra, as in Shubra, Christians and Muslims, mosques and churches co-exist. Since the early seventies, the tension between religious groups has grown gradually more bitter, with minor disputes between neighbors constantly posing the risk of religious strife. Nevertheless, on that June evening in 1981, when the Coptic owner of a small piece of land he had been given by the administration to store goods, accompanied by Muslim acquaintances, walked toward other Muslims, fundamentalists, who had been occupying the land for several days proclaiming that they wanted to build a mosque there, the atmosphere was not one of religious warfare. It was simply a matter of enforcing respect for the rights of a neighborhood resident that were threatened by a group from another neighborhood.

But the owner—a man from the south where everyone is always armed—shot into the crowd. To get away from the crowd was the purpose, according to his supporters. To "Kill Muslims at prayer," according to Islamic fundamentalist militants in the surrounding neighborhoods, from which a crowd headed toward Zawiyya al-Hamra "to save Islam."

No one will ever know who began the disturbance, nor how, nor why, nor whether anyone was killed, or only wounded, at the beginning. A full scale battle, which soon turned into a religious massacre, got under way, ebbing and flowing in the course of three or four days, while the police forces were very observant but completely inactive. The police general Nabawi Ismail, an unscrupulous character who was notoriously hostile to the Copts, had been appointed Minister of the Interior by Sadat. As soon as Mubarak became president, he fired Ismail. Historians will have to determine whether Nabawi Ismail allowed the Zawiyya affair to fester in order to have a pretext to arrestan unprecedented number of Islamic extremists in the capital or whether, on the contrary, he wanted to win them over by turning over to them a few Coptic victims.

In any event, it was a bloodbath. When I went to Zawiyya al-Hamra, on the second night of this Eastern Saint Bartholomew's massacre, having been alerted by a Muslim friend, several dozen people had already been killed or wounded. Typical Egyptian mourning cries could be heard from houses without electricity. For the first time in a very long time, perhaps for the first time in centuries, Muslims had fallen to "Christian" bullets, since the Copts, against custom, had defended themselves. It should be noted that the Islamic fundamentalists, drawing with them a large group of Muslims who really believed that the *umma* was threatened, or who were simply attracted by opportunities for looting, went to work with a vengeance: apartments were burned with the doors barricaded so that the Christian inhabitants would burn alive, Coptic children were thrown through windows, stores and their proprietors were disembowelled, passers-by identified as Christians because of their tatoos or identity papers were immediately killed, churches were destroyed. When the Interior Minister finally called out the riot brigade, it was only a matter of preventing the disorder from reaching the surrounding neighborhoods, perhaps the capital as a whole, or even the rest of the country.

In the interval, I had been detained by the police as I was leaving Zawiyya al-Hamra and was led to the nearest police station, where I spent most of the night awaiting release. In an atmosphere of indescribable uproar, in the midst of tearful Coptic families, adolescent Muslim looters arrested in the act (including off–duty soldiers), in the midst of informers and police officers and patrolmen in their summer uniforms, whose white color was rather tarnished, I spent several very instructive hours, thanks to things I involuntarily overheard, with everyone presenting his version of the facts at the top of his lungs. Finally, the general–minister, informed by telephone, ordered my release, with this warning conveyed by a police officer: "What is happening here has nothing to do with foreign journalists, who feel obliged to make a mountain out of every molehill." I heard the same kind of "candid" language a few months later from the press officer of the Egyptian embassy in Paris: "If you hadn't talked so much about that Coptic business, no one would ever have known about it, and I would not have been criticized by so many of your readers." Punishing the messenger.

After the events of Zawiyya al–Hamra, in the course of which slogans that were violently hostile to Sadat had been shouted by fundamentalist groups, the Ra'is knew without doubt that his policy of simultaneous conciliation, complicity, and double-dealing with the fundamentalist movement had totally failed. No doubt he then saw his death face to face. To remove the vision, the troubled leader chose the drug of anger. But as Omar Tilmisani, a lawyer steeped in piety who in his old age had become the supreme guide of the Muslim Brotherhood, observed at the time: "Fear was henceforth at his side."

The last summer of the Ra'is must have been terrible. Even President Reagan dismissed his plans for restoring peace in the Near East.

In September 1981 began the maelstrom of arrests on all sides, dismissal and expulsions, that was to be closed only by the death of the Ra'is on October 6. In mid–September, between the expulsion of the Soviet ambassador and the dismissal of the Information Minister, my career as a correspondent in Egypt was put to an end by Sadat. Without warning, I was expelled for "propagation of false reports," the falsest (I was told) being to assert the presence of fundamentalists in the army.[2] This was shortly to be proved when Sadat, head of the armed forces, died at the hands of his soldiers during the "Victory" parade, exclaiming: "It's incredible!"

Attacks against Christians and their churches had sharply accelerated from the summer of 1980 to the summer of 1981, as though the Muslim extremists wanted to aggravate further the relations between the Ra'is and the Patriarch; the latter, during this time, although not publicly, was vigorously protesting against the government's inertia, against the release of Islamic militants who had been caught in the act of committing anti-Coptic attacks, and against the increase in bureaucratic harassment in the relations between church and state. Despite a moving patriarchal declaration that "a Christian should not shoot others even to defend himself," Shenuda III was among the first to feel the wrath of Sadat. On September 5, at the conclusion of a furious three-hour broadcast speech before both houses of the congress, in the course of which he had attacked everyone, the Ra'is announced that he was revoking the presidentialdecree that had recognized the election of the Patriarch in 1971. The Patriarch was conducted under guard to a monastery in the Western Desert. By silencing protest, Sadat seems to have believed that he could destroy the evil that came from the fundamentalist movement alone. What had disturbed him more than anything else was that, no doubt for the first time since the last great Coptic revolt against the Muslim occupier in 831, the Christians, or some of them, particularly the young who enthusiastically supported Shenuda, refused to resemble the definition that an anonymous Arab manuscript of 1629 places in the mouth of an emir describing a Coptic official: "This Christian is better for us than the Muslims, because he despises himself, knowing that he is a contemptible protected person (*dhimmi*) and because he fears for himself and for his religion."[3]

The third Ra'is, Hosni Mubarak, is certainly of a more secular disposition than Anwar al-Sadat, and no doubt the fundamentalist demagogy into which Sadat enthusiastically launched himself is not in his style. Nevertheless, at the beginning of his reign, he did not seize the opportunity he was offered to try to destroy the hateful tradition of the double standard. Sadat had bequeathed to him some 1500 newly confined political prisoners, the majority of them Islamic activists, a few communists and liberals, and approximately 150 Copts, among them a pope, eight bishops, and thirteen priests, all of whom, guilty only of having rejected fundamentalist violence by speech, fasting, and prayer, had notoriously been arrested only to balance, for Muslim public opinion, the arrests made in fundamentalist circles. The regime could reproach the Marxists and the liberals with their attempts at an alliance with the Muslim Brotherhood and other extremists of the same stripe, who had been responsible for an uninterrupted sequence of incidents of religious strife, often bloody, that had taken place in the Nile valley between 1977 and 1981.

Shortly after his accession to the presidency in the autumn of 1981, Sadat freed the communists, the liberals, and even a substantial member of the fundamentalists—including Shaykh Tilmisani, head of the Muslim Brotherhood, and Shaykh Kishk, a virulent popular preacher—leaving the Patriarch cloistered under heavy guard in the Sahara, even after the Egyptian Council of State (which contains its share of fundamentalist jurists, who no doubt wanted to torment the Ra'is, much more interesting to them than the Patriarch) had rejected, as "not supported by evidence," the arguments proposed by the government to justify Shenuda III's confinement, namely "breach of national unity," "inciting hatred of the regime," "inciting to violence," and the "use of religion for political ends." From then on, how could the Christians, deprived of their spiritual guide by a flagrant injustice, possibly respond to the appeal of the third Ra'is: "Let us all struggle together against the power of darkness and obscurantism"? At approximately the same time, the tribunal of Bani-Suwayf, south of Cairo, as though in defiance, decided for the first time in a century in Egypt to sentence a thief to having his hand cut off. Consulted, the Constitutional Court in Cairo responded: "Apply the rule set forth by God."[4]

Despite his changes in policy, Mubarak seems to have inherited his predecessor's grievances against Shenuda III; he has not forgiven him for intervening on the particularly delicate question of the *sharia*. Of course, Mubarak is not personally in favor of the pure and simple application of Koranic law, but like many other moderate Egyptian Muslims who have been accustomed to the effacement of the Copts for more than a thousand years, he has been psychologically shocked by this uncommon Patriarch who has spoken to the Ra'is almost as an equal and to his Muslim compatriots as a full equal. Now,according to popular wisdom, "there cannot be two Pharaohs in Egypt." It is absurd to claim that Shenuda III had political ambitions, even if he has political intelligence, unlike most of his predecessors who were without the talent to stir up people and ideas. When Sadat's plan to return to complete Muslim law, prepared to please the fundamentalists, began to take on concrete form after 1975, the Patriarch decided to step into the breach to prevent the already distressing situation of his flock from deteriorating even further.

Shenuda III was placed on the patriarchal throne in 1971, at the age of forty–eight, by the hand of a child who chose one of the three ballots on which the bishops had written three of their names. His name was Nazir Gayed, and he no doubt chose his religious name when he entered orders by reference to Saint Chenouda the Great, one of the glories of old fighting Christianity in Egypt. He was a former monk, like all Orthodox Coptic prelates. Since celibacy is required, according to the Alexandrian tradition, for the popes and leaders of dioceses, while simple priests, on the contrary, are supposed to be married, the upper hierarchy can only be of monastic origin. Although the human and geopolitical contexts are rather different, in the Nile valley as in the mountains of Lebanon, the spirit of Christianity was preserved in the monasteries.

Born in 1923 in the harsh region of Upper Egypt, with its bandits, hereditary feuds, and above all the highest concentration of Copts in the whole valley, the future patriarch came from a rural middle class family (like Sadat and Mubarak) and he spent his youth in an atmosphere of permanent psychological alert. A reserve officer, a journalist, even an occasional poet, with degrees in literature, archeology, and theology, Shenuda was immersed in his century before leaving it in 1954 to enter the monastery known as the monastery of the Syrians, in Wadi Natron in the midst of the western desert. Preferring a cave in the Sahara surrounding his cell, the young monk spent several years meditating on the Scriptures and the writings of the Church Fathers, but also on the present situation of the Copts.

Finally drawn out of his meditations by the Patriarch Cyril VI, who needed a secretary versed in worldly matters as well as religious ones, he was anointed as a bishop in 1962 and placed in charge of education in the patriarchate, which allowed him to draw up a catalogue of the discriminations suffered by the Copts in this domain. With complete command of Classical Arabic and a thorough knowledge of the Koran, Shenuda felt more than others the absurdity and injustice of the, naturally unwritten, rule, beginning with Nasser, according to which Copts could no longer teach Arabic.

Victim first of all of a Sadat who was unable to understand the phenomenal change in the history of Egypt represented by the refusal of a Coptic prelate to see his community suffer the humiliations inflicted by Muslim fundamentalists in silence, Shenuda III later suffered from the cowardice of a Mubarak who, not daring to decide to replace the fallen Patriarch on his throne, pretended to believe that he was keeping him captive to protect him from possible fundamentalist vengeance. The prisoner, who was allowed to see almost no one, except for his lawyer and presidential envoys who came to ask him to abdicate formally so that a new, more docile, patriarch could be elected, had ample time to meditate on how dangerous it was to try to change Egypt into a country that was as friendly to its Christians as to its Muslims.

In June 1967, in the disarray that seized the peoples of the southern arc of the Mediterranean after the third Arab defeat at the hands of Israel, the believers, that is, the immense majority of the population of the region, gave themselves a strong injection of religion, the only basic ingredient that had survived from the bankruptcy into which, even before the military defeat, the ruling groups and their cultural, political, and economic "models" had already partly sunk. Among many

Muslims the overdose of religion revived the vigorous fundamentalism of the period before the Second World War, with all its implications for government power. Among the Christians, particularly in Egypt, the revival of religion made the atavistic political repression even more painful; the "popular" compensation was the appearance of the Virgin, "seen" several times in 1968 by thousands of people of all faiths, nightly walking on the dome of a suburban Coptic church surrounded by a flock of doves.

For the educated young, grouped around a few charismatic former monks, like Shenuda or his rival, the former pharmacist Matta al-Maskin—Matthew the Poor—an entire spiritual and intellectual life centered on faith came to life. From the Red Sea to the western desert, the monasteries that in living memory had been abandoned to a few old, dirty, and ignorant monks, have been filled since 1970 with young lawyers, engineers, doctors and teachers. In an unprecedented step, the monastery of Saint Paul, in the desert between the Nile and the Gulf of Suez, was entrusted to an ex-officer who had sworn to take vows during the 1973 war if he escaped with his life. At Wadi Natrun, between Cairo and Alexandria, centuries old earthen fortifications were unhesitatingly replaced by concrete cells for monks who were as passionate about Christology as about electronics, while tractors and irrigation forced the arid dunes to become a vegetable garden.

This breach of modernity and these practical enterprises in a church that had for a thousand years been confined to its canticles and jeremiads, nevertheless allowed the attachment to questionable traditions to persist and even to grow stronger. In September 1977, Shenuda III received me at Amba-Ruways, the "Coptic Vatican." I asked him if he intended to complete the *aggiornamento* of his church, for example by shortening the mass, which sometimes lasts for three hours. The Patriarch, seated beneath a poster proclaiming in Arabic: "God is everywhere," gave me a hard stare with his brilliant black eyes and said: "No, never!" He had the same furious look and the same rapid-fire answer on the question of divorce. And yet, by refusing divorce to those of his flock who had dared to ask him for it, Shenuda III has sent more than one Copt, eager to put an end to irremediable marital misunderstanding, into the arms of Islam. The preceding leader of the Orthodox Coptic Church, the simple Cyril VI, was sometimes compared to a sorcerer by his most educated followers because, for example, he performed odd ceremonies to cure women of sterility; but he blandly dissolved impossible marriages rather than standing on great principles that cause human suffering.

If Sadat had wanted, if Mubarak or another Egyptian head of state one day wants to cool down the Coptic problem, he will have to begin by putting an end to the haunting state secret of the exact number of Christians in Egypt. Naturally, the government, victim of its own falsifications and administrative incompetence, does not itself know the real figures for the various religious groups. The results of the 1976 census, giving 6.32 percent Christians (2,315,560 people) compared to 93.67 percent Muslims (34,337,074 people), made the entire country shrug its shoulders, including—in private—Muslim ministers of Sadat. The census of 1966 under Nasser had been taken no more seriously by demographers or laymen, with the rate of increase attributed to Muslims in the course of the six preceding years being 13.8 percent, to Christians 5.1 percent. But social and economic integration and the similarity of living standards and life styles of the two religious communities in Egypt mean that there cannot be significant differences in birth and mortality rates between Egyptian Copts and Egyptian Muslims, as there were between Europeans and Arabs in French Algeria, and as there are between Sunnis and Shi'is in Lebanon. Some Arab Christian researchers have suggested, without reliable statistical data, that since the Coptic family is more united than its Muslim counterpart, Coptic children receive more care and there is thus a lower rate of childhood mortality. Muslim researchers have replied that polygamy and the "rotation of wives" fostered a higher birth rate for Muslims. In both cases, the demographic effects in any event could only be marginal. It is equally certain that rivalry between the two communities has provoked vigorous demographic competition. When Nasser, and later Jihan al–Sadat wanted to propagate birth control, the imams in the mosques preached against it, for "otherwise the unbelievers (Christians) will soon be more numerous than we are." On the Coptic side, aside from the prohibition of the Alexandrian Church—it has the same attitude as Rome on this point—against "reducing births by artificial means," there is the complex of the minority that fears becoming an even smaller minority. The reduction of the birth rate in Egypt is thus dependent on the attenuation of religious antagonisms.

But how many Copts are there? I will not follow those among them, or even some foreign specialists like the Palestinian Sami al–Dib Abu Sahlieh,[5] who estimate the Christian population of Egypt at 20 percent, that is, approximately nine million people. While I was assured that there were significant numbers of Copts only in Cairo and certain provinces, in many areas of the country, along with the minarets, I found bell towers, chapels and monasteries. And I counted a large number of crosses tatooed on peasants' wrists in markets or farms, pictures of the holy family hanging in shops, Coptic *mulids* (gatherings and processions in honor of a saint), even in the Delta region, where I had been told there were no more Copts. Considering church attendance, I discovered the size of the Christian community in Alexandria, not to mention the forgotten groups in Suez Canal cities and even in distant towns on the Red Sea. Near Minya and Asyut, far from the national road, I saw towns bristling with churches—sometimes there is a Catholic bell tower, a Protestant bell tower and an Orthodox bell tower—entirely Coptic villages whose existence is denied in the capital, where Islam appears almost unreal, in any event a taboo subject, almost as though the conquest had not taken place or as though these inhabitants of non–Muslim enclaves wanted to ignore it after fourteen centuries.

Nor do I forget that President Carter welcomed Patriarch Shenuda to the United States in 1977 with these words: "I welcome you as the representative of seven million Christians," a statement made in the presence of the Egyptian ambassador, who could do nothing about the fact that the figure accepted by Carter was nearly five million larger than the official statistics of Cairo.

I am not neglecting the fact that Copts have traditionally lied to census takers, and they probably continue to do so, so that their sons will have some chance to avoid the draft, nor the fact that zealous Muslim functionaries, or those acting under pressure from above, have identified entire Christian families as Muslims in every census. I have seen census documents, extracted from the administration by Copts for judicial actions, characterizing as "Muslims" people with purely Christian names. When this takes place in rural hamlets or slum neighborhoods no one ever talks about it, but when it affects the son of a celebrated Coptic university professor with Marxist leanings, like Milad Hanna, there is a great deal of talk. In short, census statistics in Egypt are totally useless. It would be better to have none, as in Lebanon.

Despite all of this, I think that there is a maximum of five million Copts in Egypt. Why? Because this figure is higher than ten percent of the 1983 population and because the censuses of the colonial period (carried out, to be sure, by the British who did not favor the Copts) projected onto the current situation never reached that point. No estimates by European travelers or diplomats during the nineteenth century, before modern censuses but at a time when there were lists for the special capitation tax exacted from minorities provide, with a few exceptions, estimates of more than ten percent for Christians. It is a plausible figure in the absence of proof to the contrary, even considering official manipulations and the Copts' tendency to conceal information, two practices that existed during the British colonial period. In any event, a presentation of the truth would now do no harm to the psychological state of either community. But who will have the courage to submit them to this shock, to demonstrate to the Muslims that Islam in Egypt is not threatened by a Coptic community that is really thoroughly Arabic and truly a minority, and to the Christians that their numbers indicate that they are a significant minority but not half the nation. It should be enough for the Copts that they are the memory of Egypt, the living memory of its greatest historical glory, the symbol of a people's fidelity to its roots. "The Coptic consciousness identifies itself with the continuity of Egypt." (Georges Henein, 1972.)

However, the most difficult task would remain to be accomplished: to go beyond the religious complex that has gripped Egypt like a permanent curse. At the end of the last chapter, I set out a few elementary practical measures that could be taken to prepare the ground. But it is probable that real transcendence of the religious question will only take place after a national ordeal, a mobilization for a "great argument," as DeGaulle would have said. In Lebanon, the war with the Palestinians ("with" in the sense of "against" and of "together") has perhaps begun the process which will one day lead, if Muslim fundmentalism does not get involved, to secularization of the Lebanese nation.

In Egypt, the 1919 nationalist revolution just barely missed reaching reconciliation at a lower cost than that incurred by Lebanon today. The development had gone so far and so quickly that in 1921, the Muslim historian Mohammed Savri could write: "It was an almost miraculous thing to see the collapse in a few days of the two great enduring prejudices of sex and religion that have been the origin of so many wars and so much disharmony for humanity. Sex prejudice: large numbers of women appeared in public, entered the political arena, made speeches, and encouraged men, by words and action, to the highest patriotism. Religious prejudice: Muslims entered churches, and Copts entered mosques, to preach the religion of the fatherland."[6]

But this outburst had no sequel. At Islamic celebrations, one can still hear in the streets of Egypt this ancient and hateful jingle from the mouths of innocent little Muslims:

> Tomorrow is our day
> Christians will be our dogs.

NOTES

1. A few days before his death in 1981, Sadat increased this number to three to "compensate" for the banishment of the Coptic pope. The custom of "obligatory" Christian representation in the cabinet goes back to King Fuad I and the parliamentary system of 1923. Mubarak, in 1982, reduced the number of Coptic ministers again to two.
2. *Le Monde,* September 5–8, 1981.
3. Number 132 of the Christian collection in Arabic of the Bibliothèque nationale.
4. In the Journal *L'Impact* (Geneva, 1982). It appears that the sentence was carried out.
5. *Non–musulmans en pays d'Islam: le cas de l'Egypte* (Fribourg, 1979).
6. *Révolution égyptienne* (Paris, 1921).

CHAPTER SEVEN

The Right to Pleasure

In addition to the treatment given to religious minorities, another major point on which Islam is in complete contradiction, if not with the letter, at least with the spirit of the Declaration of Human Rights, is in the excision of women; that is, the diminution or suppression of their sexual pleasure. I would ask those ethnologists who consider this criticism ethnocentric and a remnant of colonialism to be logically consistent and regret the fact that French women no longer wear chastity belts or that Chinese girls no longer have their feet bound. If the preservation of a culture involves the maintenance of all traditions, even the most barbaric, one would have to advise the Turks to restore torture by impalement and the Spaniards to revive the garrot, for the means of execution is a part of one's ethnic heritage.

Excision, if it is minor, suppresses clitoral pleasure, leaving, in principle, vaginal pleasure intact; infibulation not only suppresses all pleasure but turns intercourse into a painful experience for the woman. The fact remains that excision, though not as drastic as infibulation, is a mutilation which means that, in practically all of Arab and Muslim Africa, except the Maghrib, millions of women do not and never will know what sexual pleasure is, and are sometimes totally ignorant, as a study in the Sudan has shown, of the very notion of female sexual pleasure. Islam did not invent this practice. Like male circumcision, excision is an African legacy, no doubt transmitted by Pharaonic Egypt to the less developed Semites of Arabia Felix. Islam has attenuated the ravages of the operation itself; Mohammed, in a very celebrated *hadith* of the Sunna, said: "Do not operate radically, that is better for the woman."

The tradition is more constraining than the Koran, which does not mention excision. Indeed, in matters of adultery, sodomy, alcoholism, and inheritance, the Sunna is more severe than the Koran. Colonel Qadhafi has suggested that his co–religionists stick to the Koran, but no one listened to him. For once he was being reasonable.

These few anodyne words of the tradition thus forever fixed this practice, which the Prophet hardly seemed to approve, but which he nevertheless did not prohibit. Thus goes the *sharia*. If you ask an *alim* of al–Azhar today, he will tell you: "If circumcision is a duty for men, excision is not only a duty for women, but a traditional obligation appreciated by God" (Shaykh Hasan Ma'mun, then grand mufti of Egypt); or "Excision is part of the customs of Islam"; or at best: "Excision is a recommended act, but not obligatory."

As a whole, to the psychological and physical benefit of their women, the Arabs of Asia have paid less attention to recommendations in favor of excision, but the same thing is not true in Africa, where Islam accepted an ancient local custom, while trying, as we have seen, to reduce its effects. Excision, in its most terrible, "pharaonic" form—infibulation, in which a woman's genitals are trussed like a chicken for roasting—is thus widespread in the urban middle classes. Women have the *sunna* (properly so called, because the Sunna legitimated the practice in the Arab East) excision performed on them between the ages of seven and ten. In 1980, the Egyptian feminist Layla Abu–Sayf was able to film the operation performed by a *daya* (a midwife without formal training), in a family in a

Cairo suburb, on two sisters, one of whom was blind. Whoever has seen this document, whoever has heard the cries, the pleas (in the name of Mohammed) of the little patients, whoever has seen the movement of the hands of the *daya* cutting the clitoris as though it were a piece of dead meat, will never be able to forget this "fact of civilization" dear to the heart of so many western ethnologists.

Nasser prohibited excision, but his decision, which was not applied, paradoxically worsened the situation of the excised. Certain families who had their daughters "operated" on in clinics, resumed the practice of having it done by a *daya,* out of fear of being turned in to the authorities by government doctors. Everywhere the Ra'is's measure came up against the *sharia:* "Excision? The Prophet did not condemn it when he had the opportunity to do so. Is Nasser wiser than the Apostle of God?" could be heard in the shadow of the minarets. Although Jihan al-Sadat, while she ruled over Egypt, was generally not averse to confronting feminine problems in contemporary Islamic society, she nevertheless asserted in August 1980: "Excision is in the process of disappearing from our country."

In reality, for the moment, the idea remains deeply anchored in the Egyptian mentality favored by the ambiguity of the vocabulary (the same word, *tahar,* "purification," designates both circumcision and excision), that sexual mutilation of young girls is physically and morally beneficial. A bloody story that I will recount proves the strength of an attitude that will prevail until a patient program of explanation, undertaken beginning in primary schools for pupils of both sexes and pursued for years through the media for the population as a whole, has begun to erode popular conviction.

An Egyptian student brought home a blonde wife from Europe. A native of one of those poor Nile villages of dried mud and straw, for a long time he resisted his wife's wish to visit the house where he was born. He was afraid that her northern fastidiousness would be shocked with the casual dirtiness of the villages—a dirtiness that contrasts with the personal cleanliness of the villagers from the age of reason, a cleanliness which, according to the Sunna, "is a part of religion," but which is not at first apparent, unlike the dirtiness of the surroundings. Finally, the husband gave in, and he did not regret it. There was a veritable love affair between his wife and the population of the village, particularly the young peasant women who constantly braided and unbraided the European's blonde hair, admired the delicacy of her sandals and tried on her sunglasses.

The visitor for her part, who liked Egypt enough not to approach it with the eyes of a tourist, saw only the warmth of the welcome, healthy curiosity, and xenophilia. Visits followed one another and grew longer. The husband was happy to see his wife fit in and take pleasure in an environment that was so different from the one she had come from. She was making great progress in the local Arabic dialect, which gradually allowed her to deepen her relations with the inhabitants of the village.

One warm day, however, the Western woman wore a sleeveless blouse, and her village women friends were startled to discover that, contrary to the general custom derived from a precept of the Sunna, their friend did not shave under her arms. They said nothing, but after she left they discussed this strange discovery at length. Some of them connected it with the habit of speaking to men as equals, looking them in the eye. Heaven knows that the foreigner was careful not to violate local custom, not to dress in a provocative manner, but she would not completely efface her education and basic behavior as a European.

From then on, she was observed from a different angle, while the sympathy of the village women for her remained more or less intact. Thus, when they were convinced of the "abnormal" character of their friend's attitude toward young men, they agreed, to excuse her, that she must not have been excised, which explained her lack of "modesty." And they decided to clean up the matter.

One day, when the Western woman had come to the village alone and was sewing in a house with a dozen women, at an agreed signal, they all jumped on their friend, held her down, lifted her skirt, and discovered to their horror not only that her pubic hair had not been depilated, but that her clitoris and vagina were intact, not "purified."

Despite her screams, which they stopped by gagging her, the peasant women, armed with an old razor, decided to "do a service" for their friend by excising her themselves. Aside from the fact that the operation is dangerous when carried out on an adult, the amateur surgeons performed so badly that they caused a hemmorhage from which the woman died.

No death had ever caused so much mourning in the village, but at the same time the fellahs ignorantly continued to think that the murderers of their idol were the people of her country who had not had her excised when she was a child. Overcome with sorrow, the young widower made no complaint to the authorities, which would only have resulted in sending some of the friendly murderers to prison terms at hard labor. He preferred having one of his friends write an account of the affair, hoping that the document could be used in the struggle against excision. This was not how his action was understood. The text, accused of presenting an "unfavorable image" of Egypt, was banned by the state censorship. Syria and Iraq, in order to annoy Cairo, distributed it, but these two nations of Arab Asia are fortunate enough not to have the custom of excision. Thus, a young foreign woman died for nothing in a godforsaken village in Egypt.

In animist black Africa, where excision is still nothing but a tribal custom, it would no doubt be possible, with patient persuasion, gradually to change that custom. This is no longer the case where Islam has placed the seal of its "divine" law on what had until then been simply an ancestral custom. In Egypt, the Coptic intelligentsia is in the process of becoming aware of the fact that excision is a pagan vestige, respect for which is not recommended by any Christian text. Resistance is nevertheless very strong: "I will only marry an excised woman," admitted a thirty-year old Coptic engineer. "I don't want to have an oversexed woman as a wife." The most difficult thing will be to have the Copts admit that, although male circumcision is inoffensive, female excision, which they consider equivalent ("Removal of the foreskin takes the feminine from the male sexual organ, removal of the clitoris takes the masculine from the female sexual organ"), is a barbarous act. But at least they do not have to confront the sacred argument of Islamic law.

Speaking in Najaf, Iraq in 1969, Ayatollah Khomeini asserted that "the *sharia* is progressive," and he then proceeded to give some examples: "The Prophet carried out his own laws: he cut off the hands of thieves, administered punishments, stoned malefactors. The caliph was also there for that purpose." "Ali [Mohammed's son-in-law, a caliph and chief Shi'i saint], after cutting off the hands of two thieves, treated them with such kindness and hospitality that they began to venerate him." "When the Prophet orders that a house be burned or that a tribe harmful to Islam disappear, his order is just." Khomeini also teaches us that "one of a man's happy experiences occurs when his daughter has her first period not in the paternal house but in that of her husband."[1] This derives from the history of Mohammed who, at the age of twenty-five, married Khadija, a widow of forty-two. When he was a widower in his forties he contracted a *tamlik* (to be consummated later) marriage with A'isha, who was then six, and whom he deflowered—the event is noted in all *siras*, "official" biographies, and hagiographies of Mohammed— when she was nine. A'isha herselfsaid: "The Messenger of God married me when I was six, and our wedding was celebrated when I was nine . . . And I was not afraid, except when the Messenger of God arrived one morning, and the women presented me to him." Maxime Rodinson has found documents that permit him to add: "The little girl kept her toys and dolls, and Mohammed sometimes played with her."[2]

I have not emphasized the problem of polygyny, that cliché of detractors ofMuslim society, because to me it appears not to be a problem at all. Polygamy has never affected, particularly in our time, more than ten percent of Muslims; it is often favored by older women, who prefer to have their husbands bring home a new bride chosen by the elder wife herself, rather than imitating the Westerners with their mistresses, sources of scandal and external expenses. On the other hand, it is shocking that it is considered unworthy for a "respectable" bride, even in the westernized bourgeoisie, to include in her marriage contract, as the *sharia* authorizes, a clause providing that her husband will grant her a divorce and support if she does not agree to his later taking other wives. (Twelve thousand Egyptian women have made this demand, which is still marginal considering the millions involved.) It is shocking that men have several wives without the wives being aware of the situation. Equally shocking are the serial repudiations and the problems that creates for children; the right of the husband to call on the police to bring a battered wife back to the conjugal home from her refuge with relatives or friends; the right to beat one's wife with impunity, even in public; the article of the *sharia* providing that if a woman has been repudiated three times, and her former husband wants to take her back, she must first sleep with the *muhallil,* the husband of one night—symbolically humiliating the original husband as punishment for having abused his right of repudiation.

Polygyny in itself seems to me finally reprehensible in practice for only one reason, admittedly staggering: there are no significant differences in the male and female populations of the world, but in Muslim societies, perhaps because male babies receive more care than females, there are more boys than girls, if we are to believe national statistics. For every bigamous or polygymous man, one or several others are condemned to celibacy. Their only consolation is this rigid advice from the Sunna: "For him who is unable to take a wife, abstinence is the rule." In a perfectly just society, polygyny would be balanced by polyandry. Polygyny practiced alone has at least the advantage for women that lonely spinsters are rare in Islam.

Finally, nothing better sums up the situation of Muslim women than an advertising slogan, innocently used to promote sentimental Egyptian films: "For all women who have suffered, For all men who have loved."

Nor does it seem useful to criticize Muslims, as everybody, including some professional Muslims, now tend to do, on the wearing of the veil, which is seen only as a symbol of the subjection of women. Many women consent to it, and it often outlines rather than concealing feminine beauty as well as operating as a sign of identity.

While in the East in 1850, Flaubert regretted that one day the veil could disappear, and with it, he thought, "Muslimism would completely vanish." However, it has since become somewhat of a Western fad to make the Muslims "feel ashamed" about this article of clothing worn by women in the East, which, after all, the Virgin Mary must have worn.

Remember the masquerades of the woman general Massu, accompanied by unveiled "Moresques," burning the haiks of ivory silk? Feeling guilty, the Arabs did not like accusing Ottoman Turkey of having "invented" and distributed the veil in their country. Tahar Ben Jelloun himself advanced this false historic argument during a program on French television in the Fall of 1982. I had to read the Koran to him over the phone to bring him back to reality . . . Here again, the Holy Book is explicit and does not contradict itself from one Sura to another:

> Tell your wives, your daughters,
> and the women of the believers
> to cover themselves with their veils,

orders the Sura of Factions.

Other forms of this divine order re-appear in two other verses of the Sura of Light.

Europeans living in the Mideast know that the "highly civilized" women of this region, tired of sexual inequality within their own community, yield voluntarily—if they are assured of absolute secrecy—to sexual affairs with foreigners, which rarely result in marriage because of the sexual apartheid instituted by Muslim canon law between "believing women" and "unbelieving men." The veil then allows the fickle bourgeoise to visit her lover incognito, and he in turn may use it himself to remain unrecognized.

One could fill entire libraries with Koranic interpretations and jurisprudence provoked by sexuality and its surroundings. There is not a single intimate gesture—from touching the penis before prayer through premature ejaculation to coitus interruptus—that has not been analyzed and codified by the *ulama*. Muslim marriage is seen more in the perspective of "legal fornication" than in that of procreation. Struck by the attention given to the act of love by Islamic jurists, a contemporary Eastern bishop exclaimed: "Islam is the religion of coitus." The celebrated cardinal-patriarch of Lebanon, Paul-Pierre Méouchi (1894–1975), who had never lost an opportunity to repeat to the Muslims: "Our religions are of the same essence," ended his days by saying: "Tell me no more about the Mohammed and his womanizers." A Tunisian scholar of Islam went so far as to use the expression "ethic of the sphincters."

These formulas, illustrating the fact that Muslim societies are permeated with eroticism and accept "pleasure for its own sake," are thus not in the end deprecatory, as certain Muslims have thought, whose prudery probably reveals a Christian education. Magnifying the conjugal act and its preparations rather than their demographic results, establishing a deferential hedge of theological treatises around the sexual act expresses an appreciation for the satisfaction of the senses that the West has never known. Unfortunately, the Islamic attitude toward sexual pleasure is often unbalanced, since it rarely recognizes that women, excised or not, have any right to that pleasure.

It remains true that, in general, unlike Christianity, Islam blesses the flesh. Even though he tasted the forbidden fruit, the Muslim Adam was forgiven and did not leave to his descendants the heavy burden of original sin.

Mohammed himself was inexhaustible on the subject of the legitimacy of sensual satisfaction.

> Sensuality and desire have the beauty of mountains.
> Each time you perform the act of love, you are doing an act of charity.
> Oh believers, do not deprive yourselves of pleasure.

The paradise promised to Muslims is a perpetual orgy, but with a healthy, almost innocent side, foreign to Western notions which often associate sex and perversity. The recompense of the man admitted to paradise is perpetual pleasure, with houris who become virgins again after each coupling.

One might almost say that Islam anticipates Freud, for whom desire cannot be made to obey laws, since desire is the law. In fact, the rigorous obligation of marriage, which for the faithful "completes religion," the obsession with adultery, the strict and obsessive segregation of the sexes which means (as in Sicily, where Arab influence is apparent) that "if a man and a woman stay together in a room, even if they have done nothing, it is as though they had," and finally polygyny, all remove a substantial portion of the effects of the Islamic cult of sexual pleasure. The subordinate condition of women and the ease of repudiation are further limits on the satisfaction of female libido.

Having been called on as a journalist to deal with the condition of Muslim women, I have often received letters, and even visits, from European women who wanted to marry a North African or a Near Easterner, asking for my advice. I did not go so far as to tell my visitors the stories of those husbands who repudiated their wives on a bet. On the other hand, I should have warned them that Muslim law does not recognize adoption. In most Muslim countries, including those that do not apply the *sharia* literally, adoption of a child is considered a "breach of public order," even for non-Muslims adopting non-Muslims. This inhumane prohibition is partially compensated for by family solidarity. It is also evaded, even by strict Muslims. Ahmad Talib-Ibrahimi, Algerian Minister of Foreign Affairs is the "adopted" son of the alim al-Ibrahimi. Ben Bella adopted two girls and a boy; and there are other examples.

After telling European women about the negative elements of which they were often ignorant—the husband's right of punishment, imprisonment, and repudiation; custody of children (*hadana*) of a non-Muslim mother given to the husband or his family; disinheritance of non-Muslim wives; inferiority of Muslim women in matters of inheritance and court testimony, and so on—I described in detail the good side of things, about which they were equally ignorant. I talked about the cultural history that had made Arab sensuality so intense. I continued with the possibility, unknown to many Muslim women, of including the right to divorce in the marriage contract, in case of polygamy, for example. I mentioned the husband's obligation to take care of all the needs of the household and of his wife, even if she has her own source of income. I pointed out that adultery could only be proved by free confession of the guilty or the eyewitness testimony of four competent adult males. Finally, I told them of the startlingly feminist provision of the *sharia*, which many Muslim males prefer to conceal, but which continues to be applied by custom or by scrupulous judges: the "sleeping seed." In her husband's absence, any wife can give birth to children during a period of three years without her virtue being in the slightest suspect.

An Egyptian of the lower middle class was away from Egypt for three years, working hard in an Emirate of the Persian Gulf. He returned. "Here is your son," said his wife, handing him a fine baby who was almost a year old. "My son?" "Yes, your son, conceived before you left, who slept in my womb for more than two years." The travelling husband took his wife to court where he was ordered to recognize his "son" immediately. He gracefully acceded to the order, since it came from the *sharia.* The Cairo newspapers published a smiling photograph of the three protagonists, with the baby cutely hugging his father according to the Koran.

Incitements to pleasure on the one hand, and constraints on the other, finally have a sado–masochist aspect, as involuntary as it is pronounced, that gives Eastern sensuality its particular flavor. Easily inflamed, it is all the more generous because it seldom has the opportunity to express itself. The Arab–Islamic countries are no doubt those in the world that have the highest idea of sexual pleasure, with simultaneously the fewest opportunities for satisfaction. The importation of Western forms of incitement to pleasure (suggestive clothing, erotic films, magazine photographs, all censored in the East) has made the conflict between hedonist morality and practical prohibitions even more cruel.

The delay in the age of marriage because of new constraints (lengthening of studies, housing crisis) and the periodic scrupulous eradication of prostitution in certain countries have created among young urban men a state of sexual hunger that frequently approaches desperation. The fellahs continue to marry young sometimes in defiance of the minimum age laws.

"How I suffered before I earned enough money to have my own apartment, without my whole family on my back," said a Cairo architect, unmarried and approaching thirty. "Before that, it was torture. Every time I found a woman, usually a foreigner, I didn't know where to take her. Hotels won't admit unmarried couples, for fear of the tourist police. Out of fear of being accused of fostering depravity, real estate promoters don't build studio apartments. No money, no women, no place to take one that he might meet, no hope of early marriage, that's the daily torment of young men."

It is a common legend on the northern shores of the Mediterranean that, on the southern shores, men satisfy their sexual appetites among themselves, when there are no women at hand, with no psychological difficulties. It goes without saying that this unfounded allegation is rejected with horror by the Arabs, who see it as a supreme insult to their honor, that is, to their virility.

Nevertheless, Arabic poetry, before and after Islam, owes no debts to Verlaine, Whitman or Jean Genet. Abu Nuwas, the Arabic–Persian poet "with long curls," a contemporary of Charlemagne, is still considered "the inventor of pederasty" in Arab popular consciousness, for his philosophy was: "A boy is worth more than a girl." The Tunisian Ahmad al–Tifashi, as early as the twelfth century, presented a detailed inventory of debauchery among men that does not fall short of its contemporary equivalents in New York or San Francisco.[3] Rashid Boudjedra has shown in powerful prose how celibacy and poverty naturally pave the way for homosexuality in a Muslim city.[4] Ulamas have quietly debated anal intercourse, for "the Arabs have always had a great passion for rumps, in the case of both women and boys, and poets have striven to describe their suppleness, prominence, and curvature."[5] Muslim Spain, just as much as ancient Greece, was the kingdom of the pederasts; the use of young male slaves, eunuchs or not, was common; husbands sometimes prostituted their wives to be able to afford boys who were sometimes known as "professional effeminates;" in order to force the second Caliph of Cordoba, al–Hakam, who had reached forty–six without posterity, to procreate, a woman of his harem had to be disguised as a boy; but the crown, so to speak, goes to Abd al–Rahman III of Cordova, who, in 925 had a thirteen year old Christian boy executed for refusing his advances—the Church canonized him as Saint Pelagius. Homosexuality is, of course, not unknown in animist Africa, but certain so–called "bestial" practices between men and boys are now progressing in sub–Saharan Africa only with the advance of Islam, so that Dakar and Bamako have a masculine erotic life unknown in Abidjan and Libreville.

This past and these facts do not prevent hearing today in the Arab social and political elite—furious at seeing the West, which in the past revered Greek love, now being ironic about "Arabic love"—that Lawrence introduced pederasty into Mesopotamia and Gide introduced it into North Africa. The Moroccan writer Tahar Ben Jelloun, in one of his poems on Tangiers, denounces "the brothel of children for homosexuals of the West." As though Eastern pederasts had a clear conscience.

Homosexuality is quite obviously a universal phenomenon, which takes different forms at different times and in different societies. Lawrence, Gide and others, including Muslim homosexuals, merely took advantage of a situation in which the confinement and surveillance of women carried to absurd extremes, and promiscuity among men, which has transformed Islamic masculine society into an immense barracks, have finally made homosexuality not, as in contemporary Europe, the permanent inclination of a small group of people, but a general and automatic social custom, albeit passing or occasional for the majority. "It is what is called the relaxation of the poor," said an Egyptian commentator, Mas'ud al-Qinawi, while at the same time calling down on it "the wrath of God and His punishment."

The wall that Mohammed was inspired to build between men and women has all the more easily forged a mentality, an exclusively masculine conception of the world, because several of the peoples converted to Islam by the first Arab conquerors were predisposed in that direction, like the ancient Persians "flanked by youthful soldiers, the delight of the army."

Let us grant that there are probably no more homosexuals and no greater indulgence toward them among the Muslims than in any other community, but social organization, involuntarily but substantially, fosters homosexuality. "Mediterranean man does not know what to do with his virility. It burdens him, obsesses him and goes beyond him. He therefore feels compelled to exhibit it and is always ready to prove it," according to Tahar Ben Jelloun. He might have added that the men of the Southern Mediterranean are ready to administer this proof of masculinity to the first partner who comes along, irrespective of sex. It is a matter of proving to oneself and one's neighbors that one is a real man, and at the same time, as Montaigne said, "of emptying the vessels." Northern Mediterraneans, at least in our day, can afford to be more selective in satisfying their urges and their vanity, since they have many more occasions to encounter women than their southern neighbors. This is perhaps the greatest difference between the men of the two sides of the Mediterranean, but it is fundamental enough to have shaped a particular sexual psychology in each group. The sexual practice of the Muslims has reinvented, without clothing it with philosophy as in Ancient Greece (at most with poetry), bisexuality. Not frivolously or out of perversion, but from physical and social necessity.

But the West is really wrong when it believes that this long-standing social situation has finally forced Arab-Muslim public morality to accept the homosexual phenomenon. Of course, it is much less serious in the East to seduce a girl, but both are still condemned, with a current fundamentalist tendency—already responsible for dozens of executions in Iran that "should" be called assassinations—to inflict equally heavy penalty regardless of the sex of the partner. Heterosexuals are nevertheless privileged in the post–Shah clerical system of Iran, since they can marry girls who are not yet nubile and set up temporary unions whose recognized purpose is pleasure alone (in Arabic, a mut'ah marriage). In May 1980, near Nablus on the West Bank, five young members of the network of the Faithful of Khomeini were arrested for having given two homosexuals fifty blows on the base of the feet before hanging them from their legs from a tree. "Civil law is not adequate, we wanted to apply the *sharia,*" they said to excuse themselves.

The Koran speaks clearly of homosexuality only five or six times through the story of Sodom, borrowed from the Bible, whose inhabitants, except for Lot, wanted to seduce the angels from heaven for which they were punished with celestial fire. Although he was above suspicion, Lot has given his name, in Koranic Arabic, to the Lotians, the homosexuals. Only Lot, not an authority, according to the Koran, used the word "abomination" to designate homosexuality. The Sura of the Ants simply accuses of ignorance those who, "from concupiscence, approach men rather than women" (27:55).

The Sura of the Poets, in a tone that is gently critical rather than condemnatory, confines itself to asking the question: "Will you approach the males of the universe and will you leave your wives?" (26:165–66).

The sunna, again, is harsher than the Koran, because it provides at most for "expulsion" of homosexuals. In the course of the centuries, according to the regimes, the practice has been to sentence them to beating or to death. The "liberal" imam, Abu Hanifa, father of one of the four great juridical schools of orthodox Islam (the Hanafi rite), nevertheless envisaged only "light penalties" for the "lovers of beardless youth."

This is not at all the case for Ibn Hazm the Andalusian (993–1064), in his celebrated *Neck-ring of the Dove,* or *Love Amongst Lovers.* [6] He was a theologian and jurist of great reputation among the Muslims of his time, despite his "puritanical" tone, unexpected in the flourishing days of Islam, on questions of the senses, probably revealing Christian influences. "The most praiseworthy attitude that a man can observe in love is continence," he judged, while Mohammed reserved this only for the man who had absolutely no way of marrying.

In what may be another manifestation of Christian influence, Ibn Hazm plays the role of inquisitor on the question of homosexuality: "It is a frightful and repugnant thing. Allah threw blocks of stone bearing a mark at the guilty. Malik[7] considers both active and passive partners deserving of stoning. Abu Bakr [the first caliph] had one who was guilty of the crime burned alive." This brings us close to fundamentalist Iran, where homosexuals, prostitutes or not, denounced by "true believer" witnesses, are condemned to the firing squad, stoning, or burial alive. Qadhafi's Libya is no less punctilious on the question, but for the moment the punishment is merely whipping.

History shows that Islamic societies have practically never accorded lasting tolerance to male homosexuality (as for female homosexuality, buried in the depths of women's quarters, a Victorian silence has always surrounded it), contrary to what is imagined in a certain kind of salacious or naive Western writing, which comments on Muslim sexual morality on the basis of an Islam transplanted to Paris, Marseille, or the former colonial cities, in which "prostitution and pederasty appeared only on the oppressed fingers of ethnic isolation."[8]

From the Indus to Senegal, under the Great Mogul as in present day military dictatorships, the various words designating one who commits the "sin against nature" have always been the supreme insult, the one that brings knives out of their sheaths. Finally, in the 1970s, the Egyptian director Salah Abu-Sayf, in *Hammam al-Malatili* (Malatili's Bath) dared to treat the subject directly, reflecting the daily life of the film's audience. He treated the problem with infinite tact, "moralized" it, and above all presented it as being exceptional. The authorities breathed a sigh of relief.

Finally, the only realm in which Muslims accept open discussion of love between men is in poetry, but this is also an artifice for evoking heterosexual love in front of jealous fathers, brothers or husbands. The fact remains that some tales as old as Islam, sometimes still heard in little Iraqi villages or little boats on the Red Sea, express the ancient homosexual permeation of a civilization as well as its erotic and political tradition. For example, this story: A soldier of the caliph loved a page, who rejected him. After months of courtship, he was finally granted a meeting, at night, away from the camp. The soldier approached, closed his eyes, brushed the boy's cheek with the tip of his mustache, and died of pleasure.

When sultans, *ulama*, and judges were not preoccupied with the private lives of their subjects or compatriots, Muslim populations, while displaying the most categorical contempt for homosexuality, tolerated it as an outlet for under-used virile strength, a social safety valve, on the condition that appearances were respected. This remains true for contemporary Arab regimes. It is not very different from the attitude de Gaulle adopted when one of his staff alluded to the inclinations of a famous French orientalist, in the diplomatic service in Asia. "Is there any scandal?" "No, mon general." "Then worry about your own arse not someone else's, and don't bother me with this crap."

NOTES

1. The two principal collections, in French, of quotations from the head of the Iranian recolution are: *Principes politiques, philosophiques, sociaux et religieux de l'ayatollah Khomeiny* (Paris, 1979), and *Pour un gouvernement islamique* (Paris, 1979).
2. Muhammad (New York, 1980), p. 151.
3. *Les Délices des coeurs,* translated by Rene Khawan (Paris, 1971).
4. Rachid Boudjedra, *La Répudiation* (Paris, 1969).
5. Salah al-Din al-Munajjid, *Jamal al-mar'a inda al-arab* (Feminine Beauty among the Arabs) (Beirut, 1957).
6. Translated by Leon Bercher (Algiers, 1949), bilingual edition.
7. Malik ibn Anas (d. 795), a judge of Medina, author of a legal treatise at the origin of the Maliki rite, one of the four juridical schools of Sunni Islam.
8. Jacques Berque, *Le Maghreb entre deux guerres* (Paris, 1962).

Chapter Eight

A Beautiful Corpse

The Islamic peoples, who represent nearly a billion souls, are, to be sure, the youth of our Mediterranean world (approximately 30 percent of Europeans and 60 percent of Arabs are younger than twenty), and perhaps they will also shape the future of the world as a whole; but they live in reference to doctrines that have been frozen since the thirteenth century in a repetitive dogmatism that is almost unprecedented in the history of the great religions. Muslim civilization was sublime. It illuminated the Mediterranean and Asia, from Harun al-Rashid, the luxurious caliph of Baghdad, contemporary of Charlemagne, to the Spanish victory at Lepanto over the Great Turk in 1571. Thereafter, it slowly ceased to exist as a civilization, that is, except for very limited areas (architecture, poetry), it ceased to innovate, to invent, to create, to renew itself. Even more seriously, it blocked any chance for regeneration by locking itself in with its certainties—the most obvious of which is the *sharia*—while at the same time the West was escaping from decadence by perpetually calling itself into question, endlessly doubting itself. "Remaining itself, rejecting the secular world has no doubt been the greatness of Islam," said the sociologist Jean Duvignaud ten years ago. Its greatness, perhaps; certainly its tragedy.

Today Arab–Islamic civilization is nothing but a corpse. A very beautiful corpse, to be sure, but a corpse. People may run on, in conferences at Tripoli or Algiers and seminars in Rennes or Lyon, about "Arab culture," "Islamic art," "Arab–Muslim painting"; what is referred to is either a splendid past that has been mummified for three centuries or a present which is nothing but an imitation of the West, sometimes successful but never openly recognized. There should be no confusion between a historic culture, whose existence among the Arabs can no more be challenged than among the Indians of Peru or Mexico, and a living civilization which does not now exist in Islam. "Arab culture is in a state of extreme distress. In fact, culture is not an activity independent of everyday life, and when life is broken, shattered, dispersed, culture necessarily suffers the same fate," observed the Syrian–Lebanese poet Nizar Qabbani.

Before arriving at this bitter recognition of death, I made many journeys to try to "discover" Moroccan or Iraqi painters, listened to many "Andalusian" concerts, watched many "Arab" ballets in Beirut and Cairo. I admired a wide variety of painting, like that which can be found in Paris and New York, with the occasional addition of some calligraphy creating an "Arabic" effect, but certainly not enough to constitute Arabic painting. The great Syrian–Jordanian draughtsman Ali Jabri has been able to put down on paper both the poetic soul of the Arabs and their violent sensuality, but he is an exception in the Near East.

Boumedienne's Algeria liked to exalt its "belonging to the Islamic pictorial movement" by presenting at every opportunity the Algiers miniaturist Rasim (at least until he was assassinated). But this artist was working at an inferior level, in the style of the Persian miniaturists of Herat (now in Afghanistan) at the end of the fifteenth century. Would we be enchanted by a European or American painter recreating the *Riches Heures du Duc de Berry*, Fragonard, or Watteau? Rasim was an excellent artist for colonial exhibitions, not a proof of the renaissance of Arab–Islamic art.

If the Algerians should be proud of one of their painters, who has freshness and original inspiration, that painter is Baya, incomparable in the literal sense of the word, who early caught the eye of André Breton, Jean Senae, and Edmonde Charles-Roux. The particularly severe confinement of the women of Blida long made people think that Baya was lost to art, until she reappeared—thanks to the tenacity of a painter originally from Algiers, Jean de Maisonseul—in Marseille in the autumn of 1982 at an exhibition of "The East of the Provençals." But will the three-horned women, the birds with four tails and three wings, the fish–fruits and the fruit–vaginas imagined by Baya in her enclosed patio at the foot of the Atlas be often seen outside Algeria, given what we know of the extraordinary tactics that have been necessary for the painter's works to escape from the suspicions of the Algerian authorities?

I have read good contemporary novels from Egypt, Iran, Iraq, and Sudan.[3] Tawfig al-Hakim has very cleverly adapted the provincial evil and boredom of our nineteenth century to the Nile valley of the 1940's; Naguib Mahfuz has successfully used our naturalistic methods to depict the people of Cairo; and Tayeb Salah has created a remarkable blend of Sudanese sensuality with that of *Lady Chatterley's Lover*. In short, all three, and others as well, have admirably adapted the methods of the European novel to their native lands. They have not, for all that, created an Arab or Islamic novel. It is perhaps in the Iranian short story before the Islamic revolution that one can see the most original impulse in modern Eastern writing. But this fragile shoot about which nothing is known since the Khomeini uprising (like Iranian film, which was so promising), cannot all by itself constitute a literature of Islam.

We must make an enormous exception for poetry, which Arabs and Persians, even at the worst moments of their decadence, have always loved and honored, despite Mohammed's aversion for poets, three of whom he had killed.

A poetic literature, however generous and sparkling it may be, does not make a culture. Contemporary Arabic poetry is so beautiful in its old strength, in its youthful inspiration, it resonates with such pungency in the Eastern mind, that one can only hope to see a new Arab or Muslim culture come into being with the same qualities. Poetry is indeed *umm funun al-adab*—the mother of the literary arts—but for the moment there is no sign that it has produced any renewal or creativity in the rest of the field of letters.

Jean Sénac, the great Algerian writer who was assassinated in 1973, had a habit of naming the five great living Arab poets. They were the Alawi Syrian Adonis, pseudonym of Ali Ahmad Sa'id, born in 1930; the Sunni Syrian Nizar Qabbani, born in 1923; the Palestinians Fadwa Tukan, born in 1914, and Mahmud Darwish, born in 1941; finally the former Druze schoolboy of Nazareth, Samih al–Qasim, born in 1939.

It is not known whether a musician ever criticized the Prophet, but his tradition is so hostile to them that the *sharia* forbids their testimony in court, and one of Ayatollah Khomeini's first decisions was to prohibit music on Radio Teheran. In 1970, in a mountain village thirty kilometers from Algiers, we were politely asked to turn off our car radio for fear that the completely anodyne Arabic song being broadcast "would corrupt the women." Capable of "stirring the soul," as an Egyptian woman has said, these threnodies, choruses, and endless romances, played in the past behind a screen, or by orchestras of blind men or of women in the princely women's quarters of Islamic Andalusia, and now broadcast by all Arab radio stations, are admirable in their movement and warmth. But they are no longer the signs of a living tradition, still less of new creativity, despite attempts to renew the genre. Andalusian music can only be listened to as one would listen to a minuet of the Renaissance or a divertissement by Lully for Louis XIV.

When the symphonic orchestra of Cairo plays the work of a contemporary Arab composer, the European music lover is forced to recognize, as the movements go by, Lalo leading to Saint–Saëns, Debussy following Chopin, and so on. As for

Umm Kulthum, in listening to the interminable, but always hypnotic "overtures" to her songs, one has the impression of listening to Italian opera with an Eastern rhythm.

Islamic architecture has scattered, on the outskirts of the old world, from Marrakesh to Agra, a torrent of religious and civic monuments which, in its size and diversity, has no equivalent outside Europe. The last flickers of this art, which was more resistant to dying than the other artistic disciplines of Islam, appeared in the Ottoman mosques, houses, fountains, and tombs of Cairo and Constantinople, generous farewells to the world by a great civilization. Today the term "Islamic architecture" is tarnished by the miserable villas with arcades and patios that disfigure the landscape around most Muslim cities, and whose "architects" are often European.

One man might have been able, by himself, through his faith, his talent, and his ideas, to recreate the conditions necessary for the appearance of an architecture appropriate for Islam, and not simply a repetition of the past. This was the Egyptian Hasan Fathi, born with the century, who argued, when he was barely adult, for the use of brick instead of cinder block, cupolas instead of corrugated roofs. They laughed in his face. For his entire life he was ridiculed by ministers, developers, and the other architects (so–called) of the Arab countries. It has only been after the West has honored, praised him to the skies, in the last few years, that the East discovered that it had lost the opportunity to give itself a style again, to avoid turning its cities over to skyscrapers and its villages to slums.

One day in 1978, the dismissed master of the stillborn new Islamic architecture, in his old and simple house in Cairo, said with unutterable sadness: "Instead of super–fellahs, we have created sub–effendis,[5] we have manufactured sub–Americans. The rural style has disappeared from houses. Villages have become sub–cities. What people now dare to call architecture here would not even be military music compared to real music, but a cracked record making all music hateful. True architects must be musical." A single glance at modern Arab cities —Beirut, Cairo, Casablanca, Baghdad, or Jidda—is enough to show that cracked records are played everywhere.

As for Arab cinema, which in the sixties raised hope for the birth of a great popular "Islamic" art of quality, a factor of psychological release and social modernization, perhaps the point of departure for a genuine Arab creative contribution, twenty years later it has (practically everywhere) succumbed to the blows of censorship, at first political, then, with the rise of Islamic fundamentalism, more and more often religious and sometimes even racial.

Of Lebanese origin, but thoroughly Egyptianized, Yusuf Shahin is the only Arab film maker of international stature. Although he is not a Marxist, he was the first well known Egyptian intellectual and one of the few to join the communist–leaning opposition party, the Progressive Union. He approved the movement's condemnation of the Camp David agreements in 1978. He had finished and made public, before Sadat's journey to Jerusalem in November 1977, the scenario for his film *Alexandrie, pourquoi?* in which appear, notably, a family of Arab Christians, and lovers who are respectively Jewish and Muslim.

When the film was released it conquered the European critics and won the special jury prize at the 29th Berlin Festival. In the Arab world, the barriers went up. In Algiers, even though the production of the film had been partly financed by Algerian radio and television, it was not released in commercial circuits, the Algerians having discovered to their dismay that the "only great Arab film maker," whom they had until then blindly admired, was a Christian (*Alexandrie, pourquoi?* is an autobiographical film). In Baghdad, where the Ba'ath party is perfectly willing to recognize a native Christian as an Arab (it is enough that he speak Arabic), and where Shahin was covered with kisses and honors at the Palestinian Film Festival on the banks of the Tigris in the spring of 1980, there was no question either of showing to the Iraqi public the work into which the film maker had put more of himself than in any other. The sub–plot of the film, a love story between a Muslim man and a Jewish woman, might have appeared as an allegory of the Arab–Jewish, or if one prefers Islamic–Jewish, reconciliation begun by Sadat.

The reaction in Syria was worthy of South Africa. Nagah al–Attar, President Asad's Minister of Culture, a Sunni Muslim, had appeared as a heroine of feminine emancipation ever since her return from study in Europe when she had refused to hide her hair under a scarf. Her brother, Isam al–Attar, future head of the Syrian Muslim Brotherhood, had then cursed her forever. After seeing *Alexandrie, pourquoi?* Nagah al–Attar, said to Yusuf Shahin with complete seriousness: "There is something that jars in your film. Why is the Muslim man so dark, while the Jewish woman has such white skin?" (They were the Egyptian actors Ahmad Zaki and Najwa Fathi.) The film maker was speechless. And the Syrians did not see the film.

This is only one example among many of the wall of stupidity, recently reinforced by fundamentalism, that Arab film makers who have already "arrived" confront. Then what can be said about younger film makers? Most of them, unless they decide to live and work in the West, become discouraged or pervert their talent in the service of a cinema worthy of the Italian *fumetti* of the fifties, and they are not bothered by the censors. Shahin was born in 1926. All those who might have followed his path have given up. The birth of an Arabic school of film making appears to have been abandoned *sine die*, despite a few signs of hope in the Maghreb and Lebanon, which can be annihilated at any moment by a variety of forms of censorship.

A number of Islamic theorists constantly criticize nineteenth century colonization for having destroyed Arab civilization. The criticism would be more accurately addressed to Euoprean behavior toward several Amerindian cultures. But what could be destroyed in countries like Egypt, Tunisia, and Morocco, where the same sclerotic instruction had been mechanically dispensed to students for centuries? What could be destroyed in a country like Algeria, which had never had a Muslim university, which had lost even the memory (later restored to it by French excavations) of its glorious days under the banner of Islam, and which, when the French invaded in 1830, was vegetating under the iron rule of a Turkish–

speaking administration whose only concern was to collect taxes?

Abd al-Qadir, the poet, no doubt revealed himself as a statesman and warrior only in reaction to the French invasion. This admirable figure, both faithful to his identity and open to modernity, has unfortunately been ruined by Algerian "revolutionary" hagiography. The result has been the creation of a kind of untouchable saint, a bearded Joan of Arc of Islam, whose realism (his recognition of the French presence in Algeria) has been blurred, like his originality. Thus, Bruno Etienne, a specialist in the Maghrib, was forced to present his findings about Abd al-Qadir's freemasonary in Princeton in 1982. This affiliation, for which Etienne had produced substantial documentation from masonic lodges in Alexandria and Paris during the Second Empire, was considered so "catastrophic" by the "ideologues" of Algiers, that no French institution dared to offer a forum for his presentation.

For the last twenty years, the leaders and the intellectuals of the Arab countries of the Mediterranean have lost no opportunity to remind their northern neighbors that algebra, chemistry, pharmacy, medicine, and a dozen other reputedly western sciences owe everything, in fact, to the Arab-Islamic contribution, and that even the Greek heritage was re-taught to Europe by medieval Arab civilization. It is asserted in Algiers that Gerbert d'Aurillac, who was Pope Sylvester II in the year 1000, studied in Fez and Cordoba, while in fact he never went further than Catalonia, which had already been reconquered by the Christians, and where, it is true, he learned Arab mathematics. "We have to be indulgent; this is their way of compensating for their inferiority complex as formerly colonized people," says the "friend of Islam." Granted. But from the height of our notorious frustration as former colonizers (why shouldn't we feel it, since the Arabs are still suffering, five centuries later, from the fall of Granada?) we could reply in symmetry that photography, electricity, telephones, automobiles, or vaccinations are the West's contributions to humanity, just as earlier Persian or Andalusian inventions were the contribution of the East.

As for ancient philosophy which enriched Muslim thought (corrupted it, according to the fundamentalists) the question of how it came to the Muslims is never asked—it was through the learned monks in the mountains of Syria. And even the scientific vocabulary of Arabic was forged by the Nestorian Christians of Mesopotamia. As for classical science, it was brought to the West just as much by the Greeks of Byzantium as by the Arabs of Spain. Exchanges and contributions are one thing, inheritance is something else. European civilization is the spiritual descendant of Athens, Alexandria and Rome, not of Islam; and the cries of the professionals of "Euro-Arab rapprochement," proclaiming that "the sun of Allah shines on the West," will not change one iota of this obvious fact.

Today, even in strictly theological and religious domains, Islam is not in a position to bring anything new to its own devotees, aside from commentaries on commentaries. Attempts at interpretation of the Koran—the celebrated *ijtihad*—weakened by the year 1000, declined to al-Ghazali (1058–1111), and since then have practically ceased to exist. Here, too, Arab–Muslim civilization is functioning in the past, or else it has sunk so low that it should fall silent, so pathetic has it become; "certainties" about the shape of the planet or the movement of the stars, contrary to what is universally known, are still defended by Arab "scientists" in Saudi Arabia. And in Cairo, on one spring day in 1981, a group of celebrated *ulama* under the leadership of the Great Mufti of Egypt, Gadd al-Hagg, devoted its time to satisfying the curiosity of a reader of the government magazine *Mayu*, who wanted to know if he could eat an orphan lamb who had been raised on a dog's milk.

After thorough reflection, the response of the learned assembly arrived:

1. The lamb had not become a dog.
2. If absolutely necessary, you can consume the flesh.
3. Dissenting opinion: You cannot eat its flesh until you have fed the animal for some time with accepted nourishment.

In Islam, dogs are among the impure things, along with—according to the list restored to life throughout the fundamentalist movement by the Ayatollah Khomeini—urine, excrement, sperm, bones, blood, pork, non–Muslim men and women, wine, beer, and "sweat from the camel which eats garbage." Pollution, industrial, military, or nuclear, is not mentioned, but sperm, the source of life, is called, by the Suras of Prostration and of the Envoys, "vile water" or "drop of vile water," we are reminded by the learned men of Teheran.

Reading the newspapers in Islamic capitals is edifying, particularly during the holy month of Ramadan, because of the evidence it provides of the innocence of the believers and their interest in the slightest connections between religion and everyday life, but also of the dramatically low level of discussion. The questions asked by the faithful, the themes chosen by theologians, invariably revolve around eye makeup, ocean bathing, injections that break or do not break the fast, the style of women's clothes, whether it is allowed to take a woman's measurements, the illicit character of dancing, ballets, and beauty contests, whether nocturnal emissions require ablutions before prayer, the curing of rheumatism by thirty days of abstinence, and so on. Treating all of these points of view in a liberal or enlightened perspective could only help Muslim societies to free themselves from obscurantism. With occasional exceptions in Tunis and Baghdad, the answers are always characterized by the most anachronistic observances: "The Ramadan fast of someone who spends his time playing cards is without value." "Cabarets and bars are forbidden [to the believer] for incitement to corruption and damnation are prohibited," and so on.

No new technology, no renewal, no new philosophical theory of universal reach, no unprecedented political idea has come from the Muslim world in this century, except for Arabism, to which the contribution of the Eastern Christians was decisive and which has now been rejected by the fundamentalists, most of whom are pan–Islamists. According to Sayyid Qutb, theoretician of the Muslim Brotherhood whom Nasser hanged: "Panarabism is a return to pre–Islamic paganism."

What remains of the fervent hopes raised in the middle of the nineteenth century by the *Nahda*—the Arab cultural renaissance—and, closer to us, the *Islah*—Islamic reformism? Treatises that are no longer read, a few Western encyclopedias adapted in Arabic by Levantines, the discreet nostalgia of the dwindling few who still remember the Egyptian Mohammed Abduh (1849–1905) and his master the Persian Jamal al-Din al-Afghani (c. 1838–1897)? Who knew, even in his own day, that this fiery Asian, partisan of Islamic devotion, but open to innovation as a source of strength, was, like the Emir Abd al-Qadir of Algeria, a freemason? He even founded an Egyptian lodge affiliated with the Grand-Orient of France, with as many as 300 members. In July 1977, the Arab Boycott Office, meeting in Alexandria, prohibited freemasonry in Arab territory because of its "Zionist or pro-Zionist character."

Closer to us, geographically and historically, the Algerian Ben Badis and the Moroccan Allal al-Fassi, both very orthodox reformers, have long become nothing but thesis subjects for students looking for an "approachable East." By the inter-war years, Abduh's program (which, as the Algerian Mohammed Arkoun has pointed out, is still vital), was, in Egypt itself, dogmatized and denatured by a disciple who was anything but faithful, the Lebanese Sunni Rashid Rida, while the first form of fundamentalism began to make its mark, around 1929, with the foundation of the Muslim Brotherhood. From that point on, political ambition cast attempts at cultural resurrection into the background. Was Sadat a victim of the "revenge of the roots" (Tahar Ben Jelloun) or of a "return to dried up sources" (Guy Sitbon in the *Nouvel Observateur*)? He was certainly a victim of his illusion in thinking that a *modus vivendi* was possible between a modernity necessarily impregnated with foreign influences and rigid visionaries committed to intransigent orthodoxy.

An ideal type of a blocked society, Islam preserves a specific way of life and a specific religious morality that now take the place of a culture. It has found no recipe for better human government, except for a variety of autocrats brandishing the *sharia* as a panacea for all the ills of the universe. In favor of private property, but hostile to risks in business, Islam has in fact made no significant contribution to the modern economy—except for immigrant workers—and it can get along as well with state capitalism as with private capitalism, with a notable preference for the latter among Muslims taken individually.

Another element which was glorious in the past, but is now cumbersome as soon as the question of reviving and reforming Islam by liberating it from the bondage of dusty parchments arises, is the Arabic language.

The Koran, we are told, is the divine word revealed in Arabic to Mohammed by the archangel Gabriel. Its untranslatability is a dogma. At best, one can "interpret" it in another language. Translations of the Koran are thus on the index in most Muslim countries, as are books like Rodinson's *Mahomet.*

The Koranic revelation, which must be accepted by every Muslim and every potential convert to Islam, has, we are told, universal value "everywhere and always." Let us accept this claim, which is made by many other doctrines, like Christianity and Marxism, and let us not quarrel with Islam on the detail that it is impossible to practice the Ramadan fast in the lands of the midnight sun, where daylight lasts for weeks or even months. The Muslim fast is governed by the regular cycle of day and night, and the absorption of liquid or solid food and sexual activity are permitted only in the period of nightfall when "you cannot distinguish a black thread from a white one." On the other hand, it is surprising that a doctrine with planetary pretensions declares itself to be untranslatable. This is either a negation of universality or a way of asserting that the Arabic language must become the only language for the inhabitants of the world, all of whom are, according to Islam, potential Muslims.

There is nothing to indicate that the linguistic Arabization of the Muslims of Southeast Asia, and especially of the Muslims of Black Africa, whose cultural defenses are weaker and who have moreover adopted "Christian" languages, will not take place rather quickly. One has only to recognize the considerable efforts undertaken by the Egyptian missionaries of al–Azhar and those of Qadhafi in sub–Saharan Africa to spread Arabic to realize this fact. At the moment, one Muslim in eight speaks an Arabic idiom, with the rest, the immense majority, reduced to learning Koranic formulas which they repeat without understanding.

Among the one hundred fifty million Arabic speaking Muslims—if they were asked their opinion, we would have to remove thirty–five million Berbers and Kurds who have their own native languages—only a small minority is capable of understanding the language of the Koran and its commentaries. Arabic is for them what Latin was in the past for the Christian population. Even so, the Church used an "easy Latin," not to say "street Latin," while the *ulama* cultivate an Arabic that is extremely rich and elaborate, the Arabic of the Koran itself that the fundamentalists would like to see used by all Arabs, all Muslims. The attempt seems extremely unlikely to succeed, since spoken language is by definition subject to constant modification, while the "language of Allah" can suffer no change.

In the meanwhile, every Arabized people has forged its own language, on the basis of the Classical Arabic introduced by the Islamic conquerors, by adding local terms, regional accents, different syntaxes. Just as Latin produced Rumanian, Italian, Spanish, Portuguese, Romansh, and French, Arabic has produced Moroccan, Tunisian, Egyptian, Syrian–Lebanese, Iraqi, and so on. Jacques Berque has clearly compared varieties of Arabic to "water lilies that are apparently separate from one another but that communicate through their roots."[6]

Arabic has found two ways of dealing with this linguistic fragmentation, one *de facto*: the broadcast, by film, radio, television, song, and missions of cultural cooperation, of Egyptian Arabic throughout the Arabic world; the other *de jure*, so to speak, by the establishment at the turn of the century, under the impulse of the Levantine Christians, of a medial language, known as "journalistic Arabic," inspired by the classical idiom, but simplified and open to neologisms. Taught in the schools of the Arab world, it will perhaps, if literacy progresses quantitatively and qualitatively, one day become the language of

Arab unity. "Modern" fundamentalists also want to promote it as the language of the "new Islamic expansion."

Until now, for the majority of Arabs and Muslims, medial Arab has remained a cold, bookish, official language, which ordinary people can handle only with difficulty or in which they do not recognize themselves at all. When Sadat, giving a speech, wanted his people to understand him on a particular point, he suddenly shifted into the national dialect. In Algeria, many people waited for the end of Colonel Boumedienne's interminable speeches in "fancy" Arabic to listen to excerpts in French on the radio. One demand of the Kabyle Berbers is that the Koranic language no longer be forced on the people, that they be taught in their native language, Algerian, Arabic or Berber dialects, with French remaining the language of communication with and opening to the external world.

The Berbers' demand was almost unanimously opposed in Algeria and in the rest of the Arab world. "Arabic dialects are an insult to the Arabic language, they can be tolerated only at home or in the street, never taught," was the thundering reply of Islamic universities. In the "democratic and popular" Algerian republic, the state publishing monopoly prints books in French, an "imperialist language," and in classical Arabic, the "language of God," but refuses to print anything in Algerian Arabic, the language of the people. When Egyptian authors like Tawfig al-Hakim and the poet Abd al-Rahman Abnudi successfully used popular Arabic, the uproar in learned circles was prodigious, as though "Arabic culture" would perish from this rejuvenation, this return to earth.

When the Dominican father Jacques Jomier published his invaluable *French-Arab Lexicon for Everyday Cairo Speech*, he had to provide a phonetic transcription in the Roman alphabet for Arabic words, for fear of incurring the wrath of al-Azhar if he used the "sacred" characters to write Arabic words not present in the Koran. The celebrated university, which accepts no non-Muslim scholars or students,[7] is not pleased when non-Muslims dare to touch the language of the Revelation. This hostility was so thoroughly expressed under Nasser that there are no longer any Coptic professors of Arabic in Egypt.

"It is not their native language and even less the language of their religion," explained Abd al-Halim Mahmud, grand imam of Egypt and shaykh of al-Azhar, as though Bretons, Alsatians, Basques, and Corsicans should be denied the capacity and the right to teach French in France. The Copts were obliged to adopt Arabic more than ten centuries ago, and they have even Arabized their liturgy, in which the surviving Coptic language is no longer understood by the faithful. Without going back any further, in the course of the twentieth century, Egyptian Christians have provided some of the most vigorous writers of Arabic, from Salama Musa to Louis Awad. This is not enough in the eyes of an Islam which is now acting as through purity required impoverishment.

In 1979, at the International Institute of Language in Cairo, (a private organization authorized by the Egyptian government) a young Muslim professor gave courses to foreigners in Egyptian Arabic dialect. Denounced at the local mosque, he was visited by the neighborhood imam, who threatened him with countless thunderbolts: "It is impious to teach this language of street peddlers, a disgraceful deformation of the divine language." The teacher resolved things with a compromise: a gift for the mosque and a continuation of his courses in popular language, but with a promise not to write it in Arabic letters.

A multifarious and extremely rich language, too rich in certain areas (a thousand words for "sword," five hundred for "lion," four hundred for "misfortune"), impoverished in others, like the sciences or modern political concepts; Arabic, an idiom for poetry, declamation, speech-making, a powerful vehicle for both eloquence and logorrhea, is also badly served by an alphabet that is pleasing to the eye but so complicated that Kemal Ataturk replaced it, for Turkish, with the Roman alphabet. We should, of course, note that this has not yet permitted any profound modernization of Turkey or the acquisition of a mentality favorable to economic and social development. "Do not deprive us of our language nor of its letters as delicate as puffs of smoke, Arabic is our home," argue, with their habitual romanticism, Arabic speakers who are happy to take refuge in a language known by so few foreigners, and thus to escape from the indiscretions and aggressions of the external world. For an Arab, his dialect is like a maternal refuge, while the language of the Koran, despite or rather because of its mystery, preserves the incomparable privilege of remaining infused with the heavenly Voice.

In his *Carnets,* Georges Henein quotes these remarks by Jacques Berque on Arabic: "A language whose every word leads to God. A language to veil reality not to grasp it." And Henein concludes: "It is only insofar as a language turns away from God that it can claim to serve man and to provide a rhythm for his progress."

Every language holds it own genie prisoner. Will Arabic release its genie only when the people who speak it have received the authorization to express themselves fully, each one in his national idiomatic variant, like the European cultures that grew from Latin? The primary cultural duty that is imposed on speakers of Arabic is in any event linguistic. The cultural flowering of dialects, their admission to the rank of language could occur while leaving the field of theology to classical Arabic, as Latin has remained the working tool of the Catholic Church. It is perhaps through the recognition of their diverse idioms that the Arab–Islamic communities can be brought into harmony with their century, without any threat, on the contrary, to their identity.

We should emphasize the fact that this is far from being the view of the great majority of modernist Arabic–speaking intellectuals of the late twentieth century. They recognize that the dilemma, for them, is to be understood by a very limited elite, generally stagnant or fundamentalist, and often both, or by the man in the street; but they refuse both to attack dialects and to favor them over the classical or medial language. None of them wants to assume the responsibility of choosing, of making a decision. Any such choice would, in any event, incur the wrath of the fundamentalists and the traditionalists. And what Arab artist or scholar has enough influence to impose himself in this realm? The Arabs are awaiting their linguistic Lycurgus.

NOTES

1. *The World Christian Encyclopedia* (Oxford, 1982), published after twelve years of meticulous preparation, counted for 1980, 722 million Muslims (16 percent of the world population) and 1 billion 430 million Christians (32 percent).
2. al–Ahram, May 6, 1982.
3. I am not referring here to Arab authors who write in French, several of whom are genuinely original, but they belong much more to Francophone than to Arab–Islamic literature.
4. For example, Sadiq Hidayat (1903–1951)—admired by André Breton—and his "school."
5. An effendi was originally, in Turkish, an educated man.
6. Jacques Berque, *Arabies* (Paris, 1978).
7. Even the admission of heterodox Shi'is, like the Iranians, is problematic at al–Azhar.

Chapter Nine

The Hidden Feathers

In April 1967, just a few weeks before his total defeat by Israel brought on by Nasser's pretensions, an article appeared in the *Revue de l'armée du peuple* in Damascus that, for the first time in Arabic, with an absolute radicalism and a previously unknown toughness in form and content, indicated a new awareness on the part of certain Arab youth of a group of archaisms, dogmas, and prohibitions which the defeat in the Six Day War unfortunately caused to appear as a means of salvation. Although contemporary fundamentalism originated with the Muslim Brotherhood in the 1930s, its new strength, perceptible from the 1970s on, came in part from the humiliations inflicted on Arab armies by Israel, felt with particular intensity in 1967.

The Damascus magazine wrote: "The only way to construct Arab civilization is to create the new Arab socialist man who in the end believes that God, religion, feudalism, capitalism, and all the values of the old society are nothing but embalmed mummies. All that [the new man] wants is that it be said after his death that he was truly a man of action." And, after referring to Camus: "We need a man who will rebel and who believes that man constitutes the absolute reality. We will never regret the bewildered man of the past, the legitimate heir of outdated and petrified values."

In several Arab universities, particularly in Beirut, these hopes, expressed with as much clumsiness as violence, unleashed an explosion of joy, or at least of surprise. The Ba'th party, which demonstrated its capacity to be something other than a mere tool of dictatorship, had something to do with this startling outbreak, but beyond political divisions, the article was seen by young people as a first exhortation for the cultural emancipation of the Arabs in the face of the social and intellectual constriction of an exhausted religion. This fresh breeze was unfortunately not greeted everywhere with equivalent enthusiasm. In Damascus, hypocritical Sunni shopkeepers closed their stores to show that they were personally offended by the article. More seriously, the rumor spread that the Muslim Brotherhood would take to the streets "to revenge Islam." The Ba'th government was frightened. The young cadet, Ibrahim Khalas, author of the article, along with Major Adnan Hammam and the cadet Fathi Sammani, respectively director and assistant editor of the publication, were arrested and sentenced to life at hard labor by a special military court that was quickly convened on May 11, 1967. As far as is known, Khalas and Hammam were later discreetly pardoned, and nothing further was heard of them, but the question raised by the courageous act remains.

Fifteen years later, in the autumn of 1982, a dismal Tunisia was awaiting—as though predestined—a future made up of military clatter and Islamic prayer. Dumas's books, *Impressions de voyage* and the *Protocols of the Elders of Zion,* were both published in this country which, simultaneously, created a French speaking television network and denied the feminist reformer Tahar Haddad. In this charming little country, in the past a model of a possible Islam, now doubting itself and the middle way outlined by Bourguiba, a short book, written in Arabic by a professor in the Sus medical school, Doctor Moncef Marzouki, had the effect of an outcry.[1] This outcry, with its mixture of hope and despair, corresponded to that of the three young soldiers of Damascus. "The Arab has contempt for himself and his reality because he knows that this reality is a tissue of lies. Lies of politics, of news, of intellectuals . . . Let slogans die so that the Arab man can live."

Going back in time, Marzouki even dares to attack the four "rightly-guided" caliphs, successors of Mohammed, whom the entire Arab world, from schoolteachers to mosque preachers, has generally agreed to revere without qualification, even though three of these "sovereign successors" were assassinated in the midst of obscure intrigues: "Our past has been a series of plots and wars. It began with the assassination of Omar, and continued with those of Uthman, Ali, and Husayn . . . It was a period of slavery and tyranny. We are almost completely ignorant about those who were oppressed, crucified and murdered to keep the face of truth from being revealed."

This university professor, whose frankness is unusual in the contemporary Arab world, even attacks the most solid taboos. He declines to conceal what the Arabs owe, in terms of civilization, to the Hindus, the Persians, or the Greeks. He disposes of the pious legend that the West owes its Renaissance to the Arabs: "The West progressed thanks to its own genius, and this was sometimes accomplished by rejection of the Arab–Muslim heritage or by going beyond it." Deterred by no sacrilege, Marzouki goes so far as to recognize that "the situation [of the Arabs] was not made worse by colonization." On the contrary, he says, it provided a stimulus for quiescent peoples who revived to reconquer their independence. Today, their energy, briefly revived, has declined in the face of the challenge of underdevelopment, which the Arabs blame on "colonization, imperialism, and fate," while the guilty factors are above all "thought, religion, politics, and the Arab man himself."

Will Marzouki's exhortation to expose the wounds, to unveil the mirror, to accept the gaze of the other, be heard? A new seed of regeneration, however modest it may be, has been deposited in the Arab–Islamic soil. If it wishes to escape from the sterile flamboyance of fundamentalism, Islam will finally have to engage, as the Algerian philosopher Mohammed Arkoun suggests, in a "critical study [of the Koran] aimed at dissipating confusion, bringing out mistakes, derivations, inadequacies," and it will have to discover, with the Egyptian philosopher Hassan Hanafi, that "the present reality of the *sharia* is conditioned by the option one chooses in the legal order. A traditionalist option that gives priority to the text over reality can make Muslim law an outdated law. In contrast, a modernist option, which gives priority to reality over the text, gives Muslim law a very up to date character." As long as this adaptation has not taken place, Teilhard de Chardin will remain correct: "while awaiting this renaissance, the Allah of the Koran is a God for the Bedouins. He cannot attract the efforts of any truly civilized person. Islam presents itself today as a principle of fixity and stagnation."[2]

The Muslims have many opportunities to assure their future. Although a number of them, like the pearl fishers of Kuwait transformed into bureaucrats for show, claim to be convinced that "oil is a divine benefit sent to the lands of the Prophet to restore comfort and strength to the believers after centuries of ordeals," it is not certain that oil or other natural resources, which may very well have disappeared in one or two generations, will be the determining elements of that future. Islamic faith, the social and communitarian cohesion of Islam (notwithstanding inter–Arab and inter–Islamic differences, almost all provoked by antagonisms not between peoples but between regimes or politicians), demographic expansion, the exceptional geopolitical situation of the *umma* girdling the Old World from the Philippines to Senegal, and the possible renaissance of a culture some of whose surviving elements remain splendid, could on the other hand be the principal supports for a lasting Arab–Muslim renewal.

Numerically a minority within Islam, the Arabs would have a specific and essential role to play in this new development. The message of Heaven was transmitted in Arabic to an Arab, and it was the Arabs who spread through a large part of the earth. From this, there remains a primacy that is for the moment unchallenged. Nevertheless, certain Arabs see the Muslim intellectual renewal coming from non–Arabic Islamic Asia. Not from fundamentalist Iran, of course, but perhaps from thinkers who are attentive to secular realities and favorable to a Muslim ecumenicism expressed in practice, like those of the Indo–Pakistani school, little known in the Arab or Christian West, or from certain Iranians. Although almost no one dares to refer to Seyyed Hossein Nasr, [3] because of the favor he enjoyed in the Shah's Iran, another Iranian thinker, Ali Shariati (1934–1977), remains a beacon, at least for Muslims who are concerned to bring about an *aggiornamento,* borrowing as little as possible from outside. While rejecting the idea of a civil law distinct from the *sharia* and the idea of equality of the sexes and of religions, this former student in France, who knew Massignon, Fanon, and Sartre, and who as a teacher in Iran, was imprisoned by the imperial government before going into exile in London where he died, defended the idea of a reform of Islamic theocracy and a return to the sources that would not be a surrender to the mullahs and to superstition.

"In Islamic Asia," according to Ali Murad, "those in favor of a renewal of Islam are now in flight, in prison or dead, but the seed has been sown. Advanced research in exegesis of the Koran is going on in obscurity, but it is going on, while practically everywhere else in Islam, the effort of interpretation of the sacred texts is nonexistent. What might deliver us from outdated medieval traditions is the 'new departure' imagined by the great modernist thinker of Muslim India, Mohammed Iqbal, who died in 1938, later developed by the jurist Ali Asraj Fayzi and the fruitful modern Indo–Pakistani school of Islamic thought."

Ali Murad, who was vigorously criticized for these remarks by the Algerian press, in the mosques of Cairo, and by Muslims studying in North America, made this comparison at the same time: "Thomism was, broadly speaking, compatible with Christendom until the Reformation, but would no longer be so today. Now, Islam is living with a language that has been frozen for several centuries, that is no longer functional, and that transmits schemas that have no relation to contemporary reality."

This is why many Muslims think that the fundamentalist movement is doomed to failure. Or else, if it continues to stir the young, despite its rusty dogmas and its slogans filled with ancient hatred, it will annihilate all hope for the adaptation of Islam to the present age.

Once again, it is not a question of asking the Muslims to abdicate their personality, their pride in being what they are, of forcing them to sacrifice their authenticity on the altar of efficiency. On the contrary, they must be urged to be themselves in a way they have never been, by applying the spirit of the Koran in its openness, simplicity, and generosity, in order to bring about the disappearance of the petty exegeses of a whole sinister universe of small-minded scribes.

It is not the West that offers this advice. Authentic Muslims have been proclaiming it for decades, without having yet been heard outside narrow circles. Not to go back any further, the Egyptian alim Ali Abd al-Razzaq, a judge of the Islamic courts in 1915, having studied the Koran more than its commentaries, was able to demonstrate that the very close union—established by the first four caliphs, after the death of Mohammed—between government and religion was not in any way a Koranic imperative. The word "politics" (*siyasa*) does not even appear in the revealed Book.

Moreover, there is no question of breaking all the ties that bind Islam (as a church) to the state, which is one of the originalities of Muslim society, but each element has to be left to its own realm, liberated from the vise they have been set in together for centuries where each has constantly stifled the other. In *Islam and the Principles of Government,* [4] published in 1925, the first modern work of Islamic historical criticism, Shaykh Ali Abd al-Razzaq observed: "The authority of the Prophet over the believers was that of discipleship, with nothing in common with temporal power. A thousand times no, there was no government, no state, no kind of political inspiration, nor any of those ambitions appropriate for kings and princes. All the rules proclaimed by Islam, all the obligations imposed by the Prophet had nothing in common with the methods of political government and the civil organization of the state. All of that taken together does not amount to even a minor part of the principles of politics and legislation that are indispensable for a civil government." And the alim continues: "We should not worry about certain events in the life of the Prophet which appear to be acts of government. They should be seen simply as means he had to use to strengthen religion."

Of course, there was an uproar in the Islamic sacristies, a tornado among the scribes of gibberish, a cry of horror from those whose claim to fame was to have memorized the Koran, like the litanies of the Virgin, or a department store catalogue.

Nasser said essentially the same thing a quarter century later when he declared: "The Muslim Brotherhood claimed to take the Koran as the only rule of conduct. As for me, I have not yet understood how one can govern only according to the Koran." Unfortunately, the first Ra'is, instead of devoting his energy and charisma to shaping new relationships between government and fundamentalist Islam, allowed himself to be trapped by the problem of Israel. And the disciples that he fostered were swallowed up by the conformism of Muslim societies, by the Islamic conservatism that has been so extreme as to identify innovation with perversity and novelty with heresy.

Freed from the accumulated debris of the centuries that clouds its appearance, Islam would no doubt have much to contribute to the world, beginning with its refreshing belief in God. I can already hear scornful objections: "But it's a primitive faith." Even so, a humble, confident, patient, even naive faith may very well be the greatest homage to the divinity. In fact, the most admirable characteristic of the Muslim faith, naive or educated, is its strength. It has the strength of stone or iron or light untouched by any crack or blemish. I can hear other objections: "Faith without doubt is nothing but death."[5] However, it is hardly possible to propose such an argument at a time when our own Christian faith is succumbing to the blows of doubt. The power and inspiration of Islamic faith sweep away all objections by their calm presence and their immense charge that is both prosaic and mystical.

The mosque is the place that best symbolizes this dual rootedness, with its worshippers praying, reading, meditating, teaching or learning, mingling freely with people who are snacking or gossiping, with businessmen or porters coming for a break in work. Allah is indescribable, he reigns over the heavens, superior to everything, but one can be familiar with him.

The Jews have Hope, the Christians Love. Neither has the Faith of Islam whose unimaginable depths are vertiginous and can provoke fear in those who do not share it. What could be more agreeable to God than to see men relying on Him, subjecting themselves to Him? This is the primary and still active meaning of the word Islam: surrender to God. This popular faith, whose strength and youthfulness are in such extreme contrast with moribund doctrinal positions and the obscurantism of official theology; this faith, which neither European colonization, nor the attraction of imported modernity, nor "progress" has been able to weaken; this faith which, with few exceptions, is as vital among the rich as among the poor, among adults as well as children; is not, on the other hand, as vital among women as among men, since Muslim women, whose religious behavior is often nothing but a combination of superstitious practices and indifference, are kept apart from religion properly speaking (Islamic faith is above all a masculine matter, in contrast to Christianity, where the priest is of course a man, but where his flock is so often purely feminine); this faith has thus given rise to a religious fraternity that has no counterpart in the other religions of the Book. The mosque transcends social classes. Levi–Strauss has gone so far as to say that Muslims "are only at ease among themselves." Communion is not, as for Christians, an individual, isolated, sometimes routine act, but the immense collective effort of the annual month-long fast of Ramadan, when all Muslims come together—for once men and women on equal terms—suffer, and are comforted together. No religious expression in the world, in India or Japan, or in the old European pilgrimages has given me the impression of intensity and density created by every Ramadan I have lived through with Muslims.

No doubt, the power of faith over Muslims should also be credited for their serenity in the face of adversity and, especially, death. There is no morbid attraction in the East for the final mystery. Nor is there any despair—the Egyptian mourners are a survival of Pharaonic times that Islam is still trying to suppress—any terror. "Allah wished it." There is nothing to add. Pay one's final respects to the dead, and then *carpe diem* without losing a moment. This does not mean that Muslims are unable to feel sorrow at the loss of those they hold dear, even though it is true that their submission to fate sometimes appears to be indifference or egoism. They have probably not really exorcised the fear of death, but they have at least managed to strip its rites and symbols of the pomposity they have in the West. Their cemeteries, to take one example, do not freeze the blood as ours do. People stroll through them, play ball, sleep and sometimes even live there, without fear, as in the City of the Dead in Cairo.

Even V.S. Naipaul, casting his pitiless gaze over the Third World, admits, finding himself in the garden of the debonair Ayatollah Shariat-Madari: "Islam was able to create a community, a form of beauty, it had succeeded in giving people a feeling of plenitude."[6] Is there in fact anywhere in the world a better representation of internal peace than a pious old Muslim?

We should add that in Islam fraternity in faith goes along with an exemplary family solidarity—the sacrifices imposed by this solidarity are unimaginable to Westerners, and they are accepted with admirable abnegation—contrasting with the total, and in European eyes, paradoxical, absence of family life. Men live in the street, at work, in cafes, at the stadium. The home is nothing but a gynaeceum abandoned to the veiled sex, which no doubt finds in this enclosed, but free space, a compensation for its inferior status. This lack of taste among Muslims for family evenings, along with sexual segregation, explains why the legendary Arab hospitality, confronted with urban crowding and the exiguous housing of the West is now indeed legendary. On several occasions in Algiers and Cairo, having to meet a colleague or friend who had no telephone, I have been received by the head of the household on the landing or in the entrance. Fear of displaying the women of the family or the modest furnishings are often stronger than the tendency to welcome the visitor as well as possible. The feeling for generous gestures has survived more strongly, but unless it is directed toward a relative it tends to take place outside the home: the cafe is its privileged location, in a reassuring atmosphere of masculine promiscuity, which is, moreover, a guarantee that the act of generosity will be reported throughout the neighborhood or the village.

In Islam, the unhappiness of the present is often forgotten because of a kind of dream state, an elusive state of poetic grace that is almost indefinable, but nevertheless very present. It means that poverty manages to be supportable, that the standardization of existence has little effect on the soul. This elusive poetry of gestures, everyday and spontaneous, expressed in the depth of a glance or the gracious manner of opening a box or moving an object, resembles a material echo of the attraction that sung or spoken verse has for the Arabs. Even in the most miserable situation in Islam, there is always a moment of the brightness of kingliness that saves everything.

This poetic vision of the world led a severe Egyptian jurist to explain the hidden virtues of Islam in these terms: "Birds have outer feathers that everyone can see and hidden feathers that can only be seen by a few." Although Muslims display themselves very little, they are, except in religious matters, extremely curious about others, which generally facilitates dialogue, provided the interlocutors are of the same sex. It is true that even then one most often confronts, rather quickly, insuperable walls, or one has the uncomfortable feeling that "mental restrictions" are proliferating. It is well known that Ignatius Loyola, before establishing the Jesuit order, made a fruitful visit to the Mashriq, where, we are told, he saw the Muslim brotherhoods in operation. I would not be surprised to learn that he borrowed one of the characteristics of the Company of Jesus from them. And to complete the circle, no Christian congregation has had better relations with the Arabs than the Jesuits, from Saint Joseph University in Beirut to the

Holy Family College in Cairo which have been training the elite of the elite in the Near East for more than a century.

Other traits that are often encountered in the Muslim character are patience: "*Rabbuna sabur*" (Our Lord is patient) is often heard in the Orient; the idea that time is free: "Time is not money in Egypt"; that one should not allow oneself to be troubled by time. "Europe has disturbed everything here by importing haste, watches, and excitement," wrote Edmond About in the Nile valley at the beginning of the century.[7] One of the major causes of lack of understanding between Muslims and our society, based entirely on the notion of punctuality, is their indifference to schedules. The East rejects the tyranny of the second hand; the West thinks its success is owed to that second hand. Easterners have fewer ulcers than we do.

The real shortcoming, the tragedy of contemporary Islam, the irrefutable sign of its intellectual exhaustion, perhaps the principal cause of its inability to evolve psychologically, socially, politically, and economically, seems to be its passionate attachment to the letter of the Koran, while if it attempted to respect the spirit, the essence of the holy Book, it would no doubt recover a freedom of movement and of inspiration, a creativity and a flexibility that have long been lost. In short, it could emerge from spiritual sclerosis and material stagnation.

Putting the spirit of the Koran into practice would mean first of all tearing Islam away from its unhealthy fascination with corporal punishment and bloody torture. A champion of the letter over the spirit, Ayatollah Khomeini is inexhaustible on the subject of penal mutilations, flagellations, stonings, and public decapitations. It is as though one were hearing Caligula, who wished that the Roman people had only one head so that he could have done with it at one blow, or al-Hakim, the Fatimid caliph of Cairo in the year 1,000, who, barely an adolscent and already evil, felt only relief when he heard the cries of the condemned or saw their heads roll. But the new master of Persia is not the only one today advocating death for the slightest infraction of the Koran. In "modern" and "revolutionary" Algeria, in July 1981, one could hear Shaykh Abd al-Rahman Shayban, Minister of Religious Affairs, decree that "whoever denies the obligatory character of the fast [of Ramadan] is subject to capital punishment. His body will be neither washed, nor covered with a shroud, nor buried in a Muslim cemetery. As for those who recognize the obligatory character of the fast but do not respect it, they are subject to corporal punishment, imprisonment, and the deprivation of food and drink." This outburst surprised only those who had failed to notice the slow descent of Algeria into the fundamentalist inferno.

The pagan Caligula could not have the Koran on his night table. But al-Hakim, Khomeini, the Pakistani officers, the Egyptian, Syrian, and Algerian members of the Muslim Brotherhood, and all those who have thought of themselves as loyal servants of God by making themselves into suppliers of victims for the executioner or into inquisitors were or are, paradoxically, great readers of the sacred Book, one of whose principal and most prominent themes is forgiveness. The characteristic most often attributed to Allah in the Koran (no less than fifty-six times) is that of being merciful. If we add that Islam believes in a kind of predestination—expressed in everyday language by the exclamation "*Maktub*" (it is written) commenting on unpleasant surprises or misfortunes—it should finally discover that it is unjust to cruelly punish thieves or fornicators, sinners perhaps, but having only fulfilled their destiny.

The last theoretician worthy of the name in the Muslim Brotherhood, Sayyid Qutb (born in 1906, hung in 1966 on Nasser's orders), in a way went even further in the direction of indulgence. When he was asked the unavoidable question on the fate of thieves—destined to lose a hand and, for a second offense, a foot—he answered that they would obviously be given only light penalties as long as society had not established an equitable distribution of goods. "Thieves will be mutilated when a regime of absolute social justice has been established." Speaking on the same subject in 1980, one of the supporters of the Islamization of Egyptian law, Sufi Abu Talib, president of the Chamber, did not hesitate to say: "Jean Valjean imprisoned for stolen bread is impossible in Islam, since a needy thief cannot be convicted, nor can a thief of public goods, since those goods belong to everyone, hence also to the thief; one cannot convict someone who steals from himself."

Associating the words "indulgence" and "Islam" now appears, for good reasons, to be a wager if not a joke. However, this connection is perhaps closer to realization than ever, precisely because of the excesses now being committed in the name of a primitive interpretation of the Koran. "The *sharia* is steeped in a spirit of mercy which must penetrate every code and every judgment." By proclaiming that obvious but forgotten fact, a simple Egyptian magistrate, Mohammed Sa'id Ashmawi, certainly provoked the wrath of fundamentalist militants—"It is a death sentence for the Islamic order"; "Islam will become an empty and obscure slogan usable by any social regime"; "the Koran is thus out of fashion"—but he also gave hope to tens of thousands of enlightened Muslims.

This allows us to respond to those who might feel that this book has maintained an ambiguity between Islam and Islamic fundamentalism, that these pages reflect only a situation in which Muslim moderates or modernists have not yet gone beyond or established any distance from the Islamic extremism that claims it alone defends the "true religion" and the "good Muslims." In any event, I take my inspiration from Maxime Rodinson, who has said: "If a Muslim agrees to consider the thought of a non-Muslim, he must expect to encounter propositions that are blasphemous for him." It takes affairs like that of Judge Ashmawi, which caused a great stir in Egypt in 1979 and 1980, for the ambiguity between Islam in the strict sense and fundamentalism to be momentarily dissipated. In normal times it remains, with the ill informed and deceived silent majority granting credence to the promises of the fundamentalist minority. One can see what that risks leading to in the sociopolitical realm, all the more because practically all the governments of the *umma,* with a few exceptions that one dares not even name (so fragile and uncertain they appear to be) are playing with fire by pretending to believe or having the illusion that the objectives of the fundamentalists are the same as theirs, with perhaps the ulterior motive of conquering them in their own realm with their own weapons. The victim of this duplicity, after the amirs and the Ra'is, risks being the whole Muslim people. According to the Nasserist journalist, Hasanayn Haykal, the fundamentalists are "outside history, cut off from the world. Sadat was dreaming." He made this statement on his release from prison in late 1981, where the future victim of the fundamentalists had allowed him, by incarcerating him for "bad thoughts," to come into close contact with the fundamentalist phenomenon in all its formidable absurdity.

NOTES

1. Moncef Marzouki, *Pourquoi les Arabes iront sur Mars* (Paris: Editions Errai).
2. "La route de l'Ouest," unpublished text of 1932, partially quoted by Emile Rideau in *La Pensée du Père Teilhard de Chardin* (Paris, 1965).
3. Author of *Ideals and Realities of Islam* (London: Allen and Unwin, 1966).
4. Translated into French by Leon Vercher in the *Revue des études islamiques* in 1933–34.
5. According to the Spanish philosopher Miguel de Unamuno.
6. V.S. Naipaul, *Among the Believers* (New York, 1980).
7. Edmond About, *Le Fellah* (Paris, 1906).

In Place of an Epilogue

If Khomeini, the unexpected successor of the Pahlavis, is speaking the truth, and if the teachings of the Koran, interpreted in the manner of the pitiless Ayatollah, "are destined to reign over the whole world," then an entire conception of human rights, that of the U. N. Declaration of 1949, itself derived from the French Declaration of 1789, the principles that for two centuries have been considered universal and definitive, must be called into question. Complete application of the *sharia*, toward which several Muslim states are moving, from Pakistan to Egypt (since Sadat's death, nothing has proved that Mubarak is capable of preserving his country from an Islamic revolution), and which is called for by fundamentalists from Indonesia to Senegal in the name of 800 million people, is not compatible with principles that have been recognized by the international community, like equality between sexes and religions and freedom of conscience. Other systems, like communism, certainly violate freedom of thought, and sometimes even deny individuals the simple right to choose their spouses, but in general they recognize that these rights have value at least in theory. Communism has evolved, and perhaps it will be able to again. But Islam? It is for the moment caught in the trap of its *sharia*, the intangible law for thirteen centuries, repeat the *ulama*, for it came directly from a divine revelation whose "unchangeable freshness extends through time to cover all new phenomena."

I believe that the privileged domain in which combat should be waged against the Islamic fundamentalist movement is that of human rights. There are those, however, who still hesitate to wage that battle, for fear of alienating Muslims as a whole. But refusing to combat Koranic fundamentalism for fear of harming or displeasing Islam would be an attitude comparable to that which consisted of keeping silent about Nazism or Stalinism in order to avoid taking on at the same time the German or Russian people. To denounce Islamic fundamentalism, on the contrary, is to encourge modernist Muslims to do the same and to enlighten the deceived Muslims. there need be no misgivings; otherwise, what we observe today in Iran, Pakistan, Saudi Arabia, and Libya—and this is only the tip of the iceberg—we will soon see in the Maghrib, in Egypt, the Levant, and Malaysia, if a preventive and multifarious struggle against the fundamentalist militants is not vigorously conducted with the support of the world community.

Instead of striving to present, in Europe and America, a watered down version of fundamentalism, the Western intelligentsia would be better advised to mobilize against fundamentalist excesses and to give prominence to the efforts of the few Muslim states, the few Eastern men of religion, politics, and culture (Muslims, but also Christians and sometimes Jews) who are fighting to spare their peoples from the horrors of the new Inquisition.

If it succeeds in taking control, it will probably become more terrible than the Inquisition of medieval Christendom, for it will be the government itself, a government that will let nothing escape. One day in 1979, in the Egyptian parliament,

I suddenly had a foretaste, and I was not the only one, of the permanent sin against the spirit that would be the reign of Islamic fundamentalism. The imprecations of an ignorant shaykh-deputy, a buffoon of the apocalypse, swayed the minds of a whole assembly of tranquil fathers: the work of Ibn al-Arabi the Spinoza of Islam, written eight centuries ago, was consigned to the fire. Goethe was right: "Nothing is more frightening than ignorance in action."

Glossary

In this glossary the Arabic words are transliterated, with a few simplifications, according to the system adopted by the *Encyclopaedia of Islam.* The abbreviation l. A. (literary Arabic) precedes the literary form of words appearing in the text in the colloquial form.

Abbasids. Dynasty of the caliphs from 750 to 1258. Their name is taken from al–'Abbās b. 'Abd al–Muṭṭalib b. Hāshim, the uncle of the Prophet Mohammed.

Abū Ḥanīfa al Nu'mān b. Thābit (c. 699–767). Theologian and religious lawyer, the eponym of the school of the Ḥanafīs.

Abūnā (lit. "Our father"). Title of Coptic priests in Egypt.

Adhān (lit. "Announcement"). The technical term for the call to the five daily prayers and to the Friday service in the mosques. The person who performs the call is the *mu'adhdhin.*

'Ālim, pl. *'ulamā'* (lit. "Knower"). Title of the scholars and teachers of al–Azhar.

al–Andalus. Medieval Arabic name of the Iberian Peninsula.

Ayatollah. Persian title of high Muslim religious official.

Bayḍānī ("white"). Designation for person of white skin color.

Dār al-Ḥarb ("House of War"). That part of the world which is not ruled by Muslims.

Dār al Islām ("House of Islam"). That part of the world which is ruled by Muslims.
Dār al-jāhiliyya ("House of Ignorance"). That part of the world which is ignorant of Islam, i.e. heathendom.
Dār al-kufr ("House of unbelief"). Alternative designation of the former.
Dāya. Midwife, wet-nurse.
Dhimma. Protection. See *Dhimmī.*
Dhimmī. Protected, client, subject people in the lands of Islam, especially Jews and Christians.
Diya. Blood-money.

Effendi (l.A. *Afandī*). Gentleman, title of respect, originally Turkish.
Emir (l.A. *Amīr*). Commander, prince.

Fajr. Dawn; prayer performed at dawn.
Fasīkh. Small salted fish.
Fatḥ. Victory.
Fatwa. Formal Muslim religious legal opinion, issued by a Mufti.
Fellah (l.A *Fallāḥ*). Peasant, villager, agriculturist, farmer.
Figh. Muslim jurisprudence.

Giaur. Unbeliever. From the turkish *gāvur.* Generally used to designate Christians.

Ḥaḍāna. Bringing up children.
Ḥadīth. Prophetic tradition, narrative relating to the deeds and words of the prophet Mohammed and his companions.
Hanafism. The Muslim religious school going back to Abū Ḥanīfa. One of the four *madhabs,* or religious schools, of Islam.
Hegira (l.A. *hijra*). The "emigration" of Mohammed from Mecca to Medina in 622, which counts as year one in the Muslim calendar.
Ḥijaz. The west-central province of Saudi Arabia in which are located the holy cities of Mecca and Medina.
Hojjatolislam. Persian title of Muslim religious official.

Ijtihād. Independent judgment on a legal or theological question.
Imām. Prayer leader.
Iṣlāh (lit. improvement, correction). Islamic reform.

Jihād. Religious war waged against the *Dār al-Ḥarb.*
Jizya. Poll tax, head tax.

Kabyles. Inhabitants of the mountainous region of the Algerian Tell, known as Kabylia.
Kāfir, pl. *kāfirūn* or *kuffār.* Unbeliever(s). Those who refuse to believe in Mohammed.
Khā'in, pl. *khā'inun* or *khāne, khawane, khuwwān.* Traitor.

Lūṭis (lit. "Those of Lot"). Homosexuals, pederasts. The derivation from the biblical Lot is uncertain.
Maghrib. The West. The Muslim North-west Africa, and esp. Morocco.
Maktūb. "It is written." Meaning, "it is fated." Utterance expressive of belief in predestination.
Mālikite Islam. School of Muslim jurisprudence which follows Mālik ibn Anas. Mālikī law is authoritative for most Muslims in North and West Africa.
Mashriq. The East. The Muslim Levant, Arabia and Iraq.
Miḥna. Examination, testing, in religious matters. Part of the *Sharia,* the Muslim traditional law.
Mufti. High Muslim religious functionary, who issues *fatwas.*
Muḥallil (lit. "enabler"). Term for a man who marries a woman for one day and divorces her the next, in order to enable her first husband to remarry her.
mulid (l. A. *Mawlid*). Birthday; birthday celebration of a Muslim or Coptic saint.
Mullah (l. A. *mawlā').* Lord, judge, patron. Esp. a religious leader.
Mu'min, pl. *mu'minūn).* Believer, i. e. a person who believes in, and hence adheres to, Islam.
Mut'a. Temporary, or term marriage, still practiced in Iran.
Muwallad. Foreigner raised among the Arabs.

Nabīdh. A beverage made of dates or grapes steeped in water.
Nahḍa. Awakening, revival, renaissance.

Rabbunā' ṣabūr. "Our Lord is patient."
Ra'īs. Chief, head. Title by which Egyptians referred to President Nasser, and after him also to President Sadat.
Ramaḍān. The month of fasting in the Muslim calendar.
Rasūl. Messenger. Designation of the Prophet Mohammed.

Ridda. Apostasy, punishable by death.

Shahāda. The act of pronouncing the credo "There is no God but Allah, and Mohammed is the messenger of Allah."

Shamm al-nasīm (lit. "Smelling of the wind" or "air"). Popular Egyptian festival on the Monday following the Coptic Easter.

Sharia. Traditional Muslim religious law.

Shaykh. Elder, chieftain, patriarch, sheik. Title of the graduates of al-Azhar.

Shī'ī. Adherent of the "faction of 'Alī," the branch of Islam which recognizes 'Alī and his descendants as the rightful successors of Mohammed.

Sīra. Biography.

Siyāsa. Politics.

Sunna (lit. "custom" or "practice"). The practice of the Prophet Mohammed which to follow is obligatory for Muslims.

Sunnī. Adherent of the *Sunna.* The great majority of the Muslims are *Sunnīs.*

Sūra. One of the 114 chapters of the Koran.

Ṭahar (l. A. *ṭahūr).* Purification, circumcision, excision.

Tamlik (lit. "taking possession"). The delayed taking possession of a woman in marriage.

'Ulamā'. See *'Ālim.*

Umma. Nation, esp. the community of the Muslims.

Umm funūn al-adab. "Mother of the literary arts," i. e., poetry.

Waqf (pl. *awqāf).* Muslim religious charitable foundation.

Zakāt. Alms-tax imposed by Muslim law on all Muslims.

Zāwiyya. Monastery, chapel, small mosque, premises of a religious order.

Index

INDEX

INDEX

INDEX

INDEX

INDEX

INDEX